The Complete Guide
to Riverboat Gambling

Also by Scott Faragher

The Branson, Missouri, Scrapbook
Music City Babylon

The Complete Guide to Riverboat Gambling

Its History, and How to Play, Win, and Have Fun

Scott Faragher

and special contributor
Connie Emerson

A Citadel Press Book
Published by Carol Publishing Group

This book is dedicated to Gibson Guitar Corp.

Copyright © 1995 by Scott Faragher

All rights reserved. No part of this book may be reproduced in any form, except by a newspaper or magazine reviewer who wishes to quote brief passages in connection with a review.

A Citadel Press Book
Published by Carol Publishing Group

Citadel Press is a registered trademark of Carol Communications, Inc.
Editorial Offices: 600 Madison Avenue, New York, N.Y. 10022
Sales and Distribution Offices: 120 Enterprise Avenue, Secaucus, N.J. 07094
In Canada: Canadian Manda Group, P.O. Box 920, Station U, Toronto, Ontario M8Z 5P9
Queries regarding rights and permissions should be addressed to Carol Publishing Group, 600 Madison Avenue, New York, N.Y. 10022

Carol Publishing Group books are available at special discounts for bulk purchases, sales promotion, fund-raising, or educational purposes. Special editions can be created to specifications. For details, contact: Special Sales Department, Carol Publishing Group, 120 Enterprise Avenue, Secaucus, N.J. 07094

Manufactured in the United States of America
10 9 8 7 6 5 4 3 2 1

Library of Congress Cataloging-in-Publication Data

Faragher, Scott.
     The complete guide to riverboat gambling : its history, and how to play, win, and have fun / by Scott Faragher.
          p.   cm.
     "A Citadel Press book."
     ISBN 0–8065–1569–4
     1. Gambling.   2. River boats—United States—Directories.
     3. Gambling—United States—History.   4. River boats—United States—History.   I. Title.
     GV1301.F37   1994
     795'.0973—dc20
                                                                94–18302
                                                                   CIP

CONTENTS

PREFACE

Gambling, or gaming, as it is more politely called these days, is a nationwide phenomenon, one which has been bubbling under the surface of America for the last several years. According to a recent issue of C. J. Lawrence's authoritative *Gaming Weekly*, only 15 percent of the U.S. population has ever even been inside any kind of casino at all, let alone placed a bet—a statistic that is about to radically and rapidly change. It seems as if casinos are springing up everywhere. Almost overnight, riverboat, land-based, and floating casinos are attracting large crowds and bringing in astronomical revenues, both for the casino owners and for the states in which they operate. When, where, and how did all of this come about? How did it happen so quickly? Where are these casinos located? What types of gambling can be done there, and where can one get up-to-date information about them?

The purpose of this book is to answer these and other questions as well as to provide a complete guide to the new riverboat casinos.

While every effort has been made to assure that the information included in this book is both up-to-the-minute and correct, the rapidly changing events in the world of riverboat gambling make it advisable for the gaming patron to call the boats listed in this book prior to making specific plans.

ACKNOWLEDGMENTS

Thanks to Katherine Harrington, my constant companion, and to brothers Bard, Chad, and Tait Selden of Tunica, Mississippi.

The national scene in riverboat gaming is expanding so rapidly that it sometimes seems impossible to keep up with what's going to happen next. This book owes a great debt of gratitude to the following persons and companies. Thanks to *International Gaming and Wagering Business* magazine, and to Dave Powers for getting us into the Riverboat Gaming Congress and Expo at the last minute. Having everything waiting for us when we arrived was not only a great help but a pleasant surprise. Thanks to Larry Pearson of *Passenger Vessel News*, probably the most knowledgeable and well-informed person in the riverboat gaming business. Thanks to Wonnie Short at J. C. Bradford in Nashville, who made me aware of the magnitude of the gaming business; Freya Read of C. J. Lawrence's *Gaming Weekly*; J. Fox of Bayou Caddy's Jubilee; Kathy Campellone at Players in Lake Charles; Gary Lipely at Trinity Marine Group in Gulfport; Vincent Creel at Biloxi Belle; Bobbie Maneri at Casino Magic Bay St. Louis; Suzanne Singletary at the Mississippi Department of Tourism; Liz Bacon at Harrah's office in Memphis, Carol Halicki at Par-A-Dice; Clay Lawson from Las Vegas Casino in Greenville, Mississippi; Lori Hutzler at Isle of Capri in Biloxi; and Gloria Watkins at Vicksburg's Isle of Capri; Bobby Kehl with Mississippi Belle II in Clinton, Iowa; Sean Clark at the President Casino in Davenport, Iowa; Brad Meyer with Ameristar in Vicksburg; Ken Wooden at Copa Casino in Gulfport; Marsha Cameron at Archer-Malmo in Memphis; J. Carroll Cotten at Casino Rouge in Baton Rouge; Al Treise at Paul-Son Dice and Card; Valerie Hughes at Bally's Mhoon Landing; Gena McCarlie and Tommy Herbert at Gold Coast in Biloxi; Bill Alfredo at Dubuque Diamond Jo.

Thanks also to James Jackson at Fitzgerald's Advertising in New Orleans for his help on the New Orleans Star Casino; Kim

Stevens at Edelman PR in Chicago for her help with the Hollywood Casino in Aurora; Julie Drake for her help with the Alton Belle II in Alton, Illinois; Cindy Behrends at the Silver Eagle, Tim Hoyle at Harrah's for help with Joliet, Illinois.

And thanks to Rebecca McIntyre at the Silver Eagle at East Dubuque, Illinois; Mary Phalen at the Joliet Empress Casinos; Barbara McDougal at the Missouri Gaming Commission; Sally Hayes at the Illinois Gaming Board, Ricki X at Casino Rock Island; John Ryden at Elgin Riverboat Resort; Judy Green at Indiana Gaming Commission; Kathy Powell at Grand Palais New Orleans; Ann Wallace at the Hilton Queen of New Orleans; Jeanine Repa at the Boomtown Belle in Harvey, Louisiana; Cletia Smith at the Louisiana Gaming Commission; Jean Lanier at the Horseshoe in Bossier City, Louisiana; Joe Giardina at Grand Casino Biloxi; Michael Northcutt at Treasure Bay; Larry Turk at Fitzgerald's; and Oswald Banks Lobrecue, Jr.

Thanks to riverboat captain Richard Jett, CSA, commander of the CSS *Maplehurst.*

Last but not least, thanks to the Gumbo Shop and Cafe du Monde in New Orleans, and Dick Lewis's Apa Dapa Cafe in Richmond, Indiana.

Writing this book has been great fun. Visiting the casinos and meeting the various people who run and own them has been a treat. I hope you enjoy this book and that you, as they say, "Have a lucky day."

PART I

HOW IT
ALL STARTED

Riverboat Gambling and Its Background

There are several reasons why gaming has become more acceptable to the public at large, and specific states and regions in particular. It seems that there has been a shift in public consciousness as to what constitutes moral conduct.

Over the past two decades, we as a nation have witnessed

Biloxi Belle, Biloxi, Mississippi

such an astonishing elevation of criminal activity that gambling hardly seems offensive. Today, in states where gaming is still considered to be an unlawful activity, it is felt by many to be a "victimless crime."

Secondly, and because of the increased need for funds at the state, local, and federal levels, gaming provides an acceptable and desirable alternative to increased taxation.

In addition to the increased revenue which gaming provides to the governments, there is another consideration of equal, and in some cases greater, importance: jobs. In areas where unemployment is high, the opening of casinos creates an entirely new source of jobs in a variety of significant ways. Lawyers negotiate terms, surveyors map out the land, and architects draw blueprints for hotels. Construction materials and equipment are needed. Interior designers and landscapers are employed to tie it all together. In addition, casinos provide jobs in related support areas such as the construction and staffing of hotels, restaurants, shopping centers, and equipment suppliers. All down the line, casinos mean jobs, money-spending tourists, increased municipal funds, and a higher standard of living.

Thirdly, gaming offers something entirely new and interesting for the adult in search of entertainment. Not only have casinos of all types continued to seek adult patrons, but now even Las Vegas, gambling capital of the world, is actively seeking families, offering theme-park-oriented casinos which equal similar operations anywhere in the world.

SOME BACKGROUND INFORMATION ON AMERICAN GAMBLING

It all started with the legalization of gambling in Nevada in 1931. Forty-five years later gambling was legalized in Atlantic City, New Jersey. Then, in 1988, federal legislation authorized the Indian Gaming Regulatory Act, permitting casinos on Native American–owned lands. A flurry of legislation permitting various forms of gambling in other states immediately followed. In 1989 Iowa became the first state to legalize riverboat gambling. In 1990 Colorado legalized gambling in several areas, and Mississippi and Illinois legalized riverboat gambling. In 1991 Louisiana and Missouri legalized riverboat gambling. In 1992 Louisiana passed legislation permitting a New Orleans land-based casino. The first boats began operations in Iowa in 1991, with other states coming on line as soon as possible. By the end of 1993, boats were operational in Iowa, Illinois, Louisiana, and Mississippi. It is difficult for surrounding states to see the success of these projects without considering similar moves, and as a result, legislation is currently pending in a dozen other states which would authorize riverboat gambling.

For years, people have been going to Las Vegas for a chance to gamble and to be entertained by the world's greatest performers. Las Vegas is without doubt unique in all the world. The entire city is one vast and glorious movie set surrounded by a halo of neon. But for the average citizens, Las Vegas is too far from home. The same holds true, though to a lesser degree, for Atlantic City, which was until recently America's other gaming mecca.

The birth of riverboat gambling in Iowa, Missouri, Illinois, Mississippi, Louisiana, and Indiana has increased the availability of casinos for a larger segment of America. But the casino and gaming boom has just begun, not only with a revived interest in the established land-based casinos of Las Vegas and Atlantic City, but with the rapidly emerging riverboat casinos, new land-based casinos, and Native American gaming.

Gaming's rapid and remarkable turnaround in the public's acceptance is the result of many factors, but the lottery is probably the most potent single contributor to the change in attitude. A lottery somehow seems cleaner and less like real gambling than rolling dice. Like bingo, it's hardly gambling at all. While almost every city has long had an illegal lottery referred to as the "numbers," it was not until 1964 that the first legal lottery of the twentieth century was held in New Hampshire. By 1991 lotteries were fully operational in thirty-four states.

A WORD ABOUT THE INDIAN GAMING REGULATORY ACT

While much of America hasn't yet heard of the Indian Gaming Regulatory Act, the passage of this legislation in 1988 legalized gaming on Native American–owned lands. The IGRA, while not within the scope of this book, is worth mentioning briefly. The Indian Gaming Regulatory Act was passed in an effort to provide both incentive and revenue to Native Americans. While some non–Native Americans in surrounding areas have objected, there is little to complain about.

The public at large strongly favors Native American gaming for the same reasons that the IGRA was passed in the first place: Tribal governments, like ordinary local and state governments, are responsible to the citizens for such things as schools, crime prevention, medical, fire, police, health care, and so on. The revenues generated will help the various Native American tribes to develop economic self-sufficiency. In addition, the Native American casinos have created large numbers of jobs already. In Minnesota, for example, Native American gaming is the seventh-largest employer in the state.

Perhaps the single most important result of the IGRA is that it opened the door for all subsequent gaming activity, both land-based and riverboat. But what considerations factor into a casino's decision on where to locate a facility?

The population base in an area is a primary concern for casino owners. A safe guide, one employed by Grand Casinos, for example, is that for a casino to be built in an emerging market, there must be a population base of at least 4 million people within 150 miles of the proposed site. There is also the consideration of the viability of the site in terms of a day-trip market. With casinos often costing over $50 million, these and other factors must be considered in great detail.

While some of the Native American and land-based casinos are up and running, the public's imagination seems to be captivated by the new riverboats. The nostalgic lure of tradition and history have combined with the romance and risk of courting Dame Fortune, to provide a unique experience which the new riverboat casinos offer. As will be seen, the size and style of the riverboats vary from the traditional to the futuristic. Some boats cruise the waterways, while others remain permanently moored at the dock. One thing is certain, and that is that no expense has been spared in making each casino as fantastic, lavish, and exciting as possible.

THE MIGHTY MISSISSIPPI

Despite the fact that riverboat gambling has been legalized in several states, with more on the way, the term "riverboat" almost universally evokes images of the Mississippi River. It's easy enough to imagine shallow-bottomed sidewheelers with smoke pouring from twin stacks, moving gracefully down the Mississippi River. One can easily visualize well-dressed nineteenth-century ladies and gentlemen enjoying a leisurely stroll on the outside decks in the warm summer air. Inside one of the beautiful parlors, rich, cigar-smoking businessmen enjoy tempting fate with a game of chance. The stakes are high.

Elsewhere on the magnificent floating palace, there is lavish entertainment, dancing, and fine dining. Laughter mixes with spirited conversations, and lively discussions abound concerning the cotton and sugar crops. Intimate liaisons are conducted, deals are made, and business is transacted. The riverboat cruise down the mighty Mississippi is unlike anything else.

The steamboat era was unique in American history. It was the stuff of dreams, a magnificent and legendary period which, like the plantation era, was considered lost forever. The passage of laws in Mississippi and other states legalizing riverboat gambling has made it possible to recapture some of that lost glory in the present.

The laws of the states which have enacted riverboat legislation, however, are as varied and individual as the collective personalities which these states embody. This is very important to the gambler, since these laws control and limit the size and types of bets which the customer may place. Some of these laws and regulations are obviously absurd and seem almost to have been enacted out a sense of guilt at having legalized gambling in the first place. In Part II, we will briefly examine these laws on a state-by-state basis, so that the gaming enthusiast can determine which states and riverboats are the most suited to his or her individual tastes.

Shipbuilding

The sudden and rapid emergence of riverboat gambling nationwide has created an immediate and unprecedented need for riverboats, barges, ships, and other support vessels of all types. As a result of this demand, shipbuilders and construction companies throughout the country are working literally around the clock building new riverboats. The procedure is

The President Casino, Biloxi, Mississippi

very complex, and there are many factors which the casino owners must take into account when choosing a shipyard to construct their casino vessel.

When thinking of riverboats, most people imagine a large flat-bottomed Victorian-era steamboat with ornate gingerbread trim and side-by-side smokestacks. Most of the traditional boats fit this description, with either one large paddlewheel on the rear of the boat, in the case of a "sternwheeler," or two large paddlewheels, one on each side, for the "sidewheeler." Regardless of the boat's style, the final product is much more than just another riverboat casino, it is the embodiment of a concept. It will carry the theme, the banner, and the hopes and dreams of those who designed, constructed, and paid for it. It will serve as a magnet to attract gaming enthusiasts for years to come.

As such, the boat must be aesthetically appealing, unique in design, and visually high profile. In the casino world, as evidenced by Las Vegas, excess is the norm. The new riverboats are no exception. The vessel will hopefully be more lavish, magnificent, and astonishing than any of its competitors. This requirement is factored into the architectural equation from the beginning. With this in mind, many casino companies work with the shipyard to give their project a unique and individual theme which will place it above and beyond other riverboats.

Since the laws vary from state to state, there are many architectural and design factors which must be taken into consideration. In Mississippi, for example, the riverboats are not permitted to leave the dock at all, since only dockside gambling is allowed. This being the case, most so-called riverboats are actually little more than elegant barges. Some of the barges are newly constructed, but many have been converted into riverboats from other uses. The shipyard must not only convert the barge into a riverboat, it must give the boat an individual identity. The boat must pass state and federal laws as well. In most cases, the finished product has to be delivered to the site. This can be a very expensive, time-consuming, and often dangerous process.

In Louisiana, riverboats must be fully operational and seaworthy, since state law does not permit gaming dockside. This being the case, the construction of a riverboat is a much more time-consuming, detailed, and costly undertaking. It is one thing to balance a wide, flat-bottomed barge, and quite another to provide a boat with a giant power plant, sensitive navigational equipment, food service, electric power, heat, and air conditioning. All Louisiana riverboats must not only pass all state and federal laws but also be Coast Guard approved.

The vessel must also be delivered on time and on budget. Both of these considerations are extremely important to the casino owners. For example, Splash Casino in Tunica, Mississippi, was the first boat in operation in Tunica County, giving it almost a year's jump on the next competitor in the area, Lady Luck Casino. In Natchez, Mississippi, Lady Luck was first. In a business where a single boat is taking in $25 million or more a month, a delay of a few weeks or months can cost the owners millions in lost revenues. Actually, a delay represents a double loss. Not only is a boat which is not finished on time losing the money it would be making if on schedule, it is losing the advantage as other competitors move into the area. It can be truly said that the greatest market share and profit potential will go to the casino operator who gets his or her boat in the water the fastest.

Perhaps the most important consideration of all, assuming that everything else is in order, is budget. The casino owners need to know that the plans which they have had a hand in designing, and have approved, will be delivered not only on time but at the agreed-upon cost. Since most of these projects are incredibly complex, it is understandably extremely difficult to give an exact-dollar cost estimate when millions of dollars are involved.

The process for having a boat constructed differs to some degree depending on minor details but proceeds pretty much along the same lines in most cases. I discussed the procedure with Bill Gordon of Yates and Son Construction Company in Philadelphia, and Jackson, Mississippi. The Yates company, founded in 1963, is one of the first and major shipbuilders on the riverboat scene, and has already constructed Lady Luck and Harrah's in Tunica, Mississippi; Sam's Town, Fitzgeralds, and Sheraton in Tunica County; and Lady Luck and Ameristar in Vicksburg, Mississippi. According to Mr. Gordon, the procedure is as follows:

"A naval architect draws up a detailed and elaborate set of plans reflecting the casino owner's concept. These plans are presented to the shipbuilder, who studies them, makes recommendations, and then gives the buyer an accurate cost and time estimate.

"If the price quoted is acceptable, then a formal contract is executed between the parties and construction begins.

"The shipbuilder or construction company is paid a prorated monthly amount determined by the total cost divided by the number of months the construction will take, and the finished product is hopefully delivered within budget and on time."

But building a casino is a great deal more complex than it sounds, and entails research and planning that the average gaming patron never even considers.

First there is the boat itself, whether an actual cruising riverboat or a dockside barge. In either case there are dozens of individual details which must be worked out. While everything may have been taken into consideration during the initial planning stages, things are certain to change as the project takes form. The exterior of the vessel is the first thing the public will see. It must be visually striking. The interior is equally if not even more important, since that's where the patrons will be spending their time and money. The interior appointments should be unique and lavish, continuing the vessel's exterior theme. The interior must also, and above all else, be comfortable. If the patron is uncomfortable, the casino's business suffers—it's that simple. How the atmosphere of passenger comfort is created, however, is an extremely complicated matter, one which has been considered in great detail by a team of experts, drawing on their own extensive knowledge as well as on the successes and failures of competitors' efforts.

The obvious things such as color scheme, location of bars and restrooms, arrangement of chairs, gaming tables, and machines are apparent to all. What goes on beneath the surface and behind the scenes is equally important. Air quality control is a big issue these days and not an afterthought. The public demands a smoke-free enviornment, even in designated smoking areas. A three-decked boat carrying as many as 1,500 passengers in a

closed envionment presents major ventillation problems. The resolution of this issue must be inherent in the initial design of
every riverboat casino. Food and beverage service is a major consideration as well. In
addition to the necessity of rapid and efficient service to a large
number of passengers, there is the problem of equipment location, both in terms of space requirements and accessibility.
Where actual casino floor space is at a premium, these are
important considerations. Let's examine the Copa Casino in
Gulfport, Mississippi. The 507-foot Copa was outfitted with bar
and restaurant equipment by Richard's Galley Equipment, of
Houma, Louisiana. The former cruise ship has a total of four 2-
station bars, including a deli bar which seats 235. Each bar is
equipped with stainless steel blenders, drainers, glass washers,
and refrigerators. Alcohol and soft drinks are dispensed through
a series of sixteen-button guns which not only regulate the
amount of alcohol per drink but also record the number of serv-
ings. The interesting thing is that the liquor is stored not at the
bar but belowdecks in a separate room, and is dispensed through
over one thousand feet of special tubing. The same thing is true
in the case of beer and wine, which is also stored belowdecks
and dispensed through tubing.

Lighting is important also, and a riverboat provides a unique
and different set of problems. For example, exterior fixtures
must endure extreme weather and climate variations. Coast
Guard regulations require approval of vessel lighting by the
Marine Safety Board. Beams and structural supports as well as
limited space require special designs. Last but not least, the highly reflective surfaces of the majority of the slots and other gaming machines must be overcome in order to reduce glare and eye
fatigue. The final result of all of this expense, planning, and
attention to detail is that the gaming patron notices nothing at
all, other than possibly a brief recognition of the elegance of his
or her surroundings.

While the laws pertaining to the design, decor, and construction of these riverboats vary from state to state, one thing is certain. The casino owners and shipbuilders are out to make each
casino project the most opulent and unique possible. The results
of their efforts are that the gaming patron will certainly be

impressed by the magnificent of every riverboat, from the traditional nineteenth-century sternwheelers to the fully enclosed ultramodern boats. Everything has been designed with the patron in mind, and the rich, dreamlike atmosphere of these new floating palaces is certainly a wonderful and important part of the total experience of riverboat gambling.

3

Publications
of Interest

PASSENGER VESSEL NEWS

Passenger Vessel News is without doubt the most complete and comprehensive publication dealing with riverboat gambling. An exceptional magazine, this bimonthly features the most up-to-date information on riverboats, including articles about their

Casino Rouge, Baton Rouge, Louisiana

design, construction, and location, as well as beautiful color photographs. There are also announcements about new site approvals, features on individual boats, discussions on legal and enviornmental matters, as well as stories of related interest. In addition to the extensive information about riverboats, there is also financial news, such as a comparative chart, for example, which provides the reader with important gaming figures from all of the boats. This chart tells the size of each boat, the number of slots, the number of tables, number of admissions, total casino wins per admission, etc. An extremely interesting, informative, and important publication. For the serious gambler, the enthusiast, or the novice, *Passenger Vessel News* is a must. (*Note: Passenger Vessel News* deals exclusively with riverboats, gambling, and excursion boats. Cruise ships and other boats which provide overnight accommodations are not covered by this magazine.)

Passenger Vessel News is available by subscription for $15 per year (six issues), first-class mail. See ordering information below.

RIVERBOAT GAMING REPORT

The *Riverboat Gaming Report* "is a monthly newsletter with the latest news exclusively on the riverboat gaming industry" and features "confidential marketing information for developers, owners and suppliers of products and services for riverboat gaming vessels." This publication is a newsletter rather than a magazine and, as such, lacks photographs, advertisements, and other interesting but nonessential information. The *Riverboat Gaming Report* is all business and contains everything of interest to the movers and shakers in the riverboat gambling business. While it is definitely more business-oriented than its sister publication *Passenger Vessel News*, the *Riverboat Gaming Report* is also very interesting reading. A recent feature about the opening of Lady Luck Casino in Mhoon Landing, Mississippi, began with the headline, in bold black type, ELVIS SPOTTED IN TUNICA, MISS. The article went on to describe developments and construction of new boats in the area. An interesting and informative newsletter.

The *Riverboat Gaming Report* is available by subscription for $75 per year (twelve issues), first-class mail. Subscriptions to the *Riverboat Gaming Report* also include at no extra cost a subscription to *Passenger Vessel News*. Both of the above publications may be ordered from:

> Pearson and Company
> P.O. Box 8662
> Metarie, LA 70006
> Phone: 504-455-9758
> Fax: 504-454-5974

GAMING AND WAGERING BUSINESS

Gaming and Wagering Business is a unique monthly publication devoted entirely to the gaming and wagering business, and written specifically for those involved in all facets of its operation and development. The magazine is produced in a large 10½-by-13¾-inch format, which is visually pleasing due to the large number of color photographs, advertisements, maps, and charts. From an informational standpoint, *Gaming and Wagering Business* is thorough. It deals not only with the riverboats but with the expanding gaming market nationally and internationally, providing valuable information concerning the types of gaming available in various states and nations. From riverboats, to land-based casinos, to lottery games, to horse racing, dog racing, and other pari-mutuel betting, this magazine addresses it all.

The business section is extremely valuable to the investor and examines the various casino stocks and their performance as considered by Raymond James and Associates, one of America's leading firms providing investment banking services to the gaming industry.

Gaming and Wagering Business is published on the fifteenth of each month and is available by subscription for $55 per year (twelve issues), second-class mail, from:

> Gaming and Wagering Business
> BMT Publications, Inc.
> 7 Penn Plaza
> New York, NY 10001-3900
> Phone: 212-594-4120
> Fax: 212-414-0514

GAMING WEEKLY

Gaming Weekly is a weekly newsletter published in New York City by C. J. Lawrence (established in 1864) and is geared specifically toward the investor in casino and gaming stocks. As such, it is arguably the most thorough publication of its type. It contains no photographs, which is unfortunate, but the information is provides more than compensates for the lack of visuals. There are, however, maps, charts, and graphs illustrating everything from stock price fluctuations to Gulf Coast boat locations to casino placement on the Las Vegas strip. In addition to the business illustrations, *Gaming Weekly* makes recommendations for stock purchases, predicts trends, and deals with the legal wranglings from state to state as well as federal laws governing casino licensing and operation. For the serious casino investor, it is without equal.

While individual subscriptions are available, the price (in the thousands of dollars per year) places this publication beyond the reach of the average investor or gaming enthusiast. Most of the major brokerage firms nationally, however, have subscriptions, and rely heavily upon the information provided in *Gaming Weekly* in making casino stock recommendations to their clients. For further information contact:

Gaming Weekly
C. J. Lawrence
1290 Avenue of the Americas
New York, NY 10104-0101
Phone: 212-468-5000
Fax: 212-468-5490

THE GROGAN REPORT

The Grogan Report is another good gaming business publication, featuring interesting and informative segments on matters of importance to those involved in the gaming business, either as directors, employees, investors, or enthusiasts.

The Grogan Report is available by subscription for $80 per year (twelve issues) by contacting:

> The Grogan Report
> 30746 Bryant Drive
> Evergreen, CO 80439
> Phone: 303-670-0808
> Fax: 303-674-3599

SPORT'S FORM'S GAMING TODAY

Gaming Today, as it is called, is definitely one of my favorites. In business since 1975, this publication, in newspaper format, is printed weekly on nice paper, with clear, easy-to-read print. While this paper deals with riverboats and water-based casinos, it also addresses every other form of betting and wagering, particularly sports betting. From boxing to horse racing to hockey and football, and everything in between, *Gaming Today* is the premier paper of its type. *Gaming Today* is the kind of paper you scan quickly but then keep around the house or office for months in order to read the many interesting articles at leisure. Some of the features are "Hot Jackpots," "Bookies Battle," and "Northern Nevada Report." There are also sections on boxing, gaming stocks, book reviews, etc. This is a great publication. Unfortunately, it is not available to the public, for the most part, except in Nevada and New Jersey, and at some tracks. *Gaming Today*, however, is available by first-class mail subscription for $108 (one year) or $75 (six months) from the publisher:

> Dirson Enterprises, Inc.
> P.O. Box 93116
> Las Vegas, NV 89193
> Phone: 702-798-1151

CASINO ACTION

Casino Action is a helpful monthly newspaper paper which is free to the public at a number of convenient locations in the Mississippi Gulf Coast area. It caters to casino employees by providing discount coupons from local businesses. It benefits local businesses with advertising targeting residents, tourists, and casino support personnel. The information is perhaps most beneficial, however, to the tourists, providing helpful and time-saving hints on getting around, including maps and diagrams, as well as suggestions and information about upcoming events and festivals. There are also interesting and informative articles and updates on the constantly evolving casino and riverboat scene. The "Dining in Action" section consists solely of restaurant advertisements, which are especially helpful since many of the ads are descriptive and often include a photo as well. All in all, this is a very useful newspaper. A subscription to *Casino Action* may be obtained for $25 (twelve issues) by contacting:

Casino Action
1042 Beach Blvd., Suite 23
Biloxi, MS 39530
Phone: 601-374-6000

As the interest in riverboats, land-based casinos, lotteries, and sports betting continues to spread throughout the nation, there will no doubt be more newspapers and magazines available to the general public in the near future. Those examined above have been, are, and shall most likely continue to remain the foremost in their respective fields.

THE RIVERBOAT GAMING CONGRESS AND EXPO

The Riverboat Gaming Congress and Expo is an annual event sponsored by International *Gaming and Wagering Business* magazine and Michael Jones and Company. This three-day industry trade show started in 1991 and held its first meeting in St. Louis. In 1992 the conference was moved to New Orleans, where it has since remained.

For those who have never attended a trade show, it is quite interesting. The format from industry to industry is usually similar, featuring a number of seminars with well-known speakers addressing issues of importance to the trade. The 1993 Riverboat Gaming Congress, for example, included lectures such as "Site

Selection: Roadmap for Success," "Keeping the Promise: Economic Impact of Riverboats," "Gaming Commissions: Taking Another Look," and other interesting topics of discussion.

In the afternoons, after a lunch break, the exhibit hall is open. This is always the most interesting part of any trade show, and particularly so in the case of the Riverboat Gaming Congress. The exhibit hall is filled with many magnificent and colorful displays presented by everyone from shipbuilders, marine architects, and cabinetmakers, to slot machine, roulette wheel, poker chip, and playing card manufacturers. The displays feature the newest gaming, slot, and vending machines, scale ship models set up in the various booths, and more. The mood is always festive, and old friendships are renewed. The evenings are not scheduled, so that the attendees may get together on their own and take advantage of New Orleans's great music, and many fine restaurants.

The three-day Riverboat Gaming Congress and Expo trade show takes place in New Orleans each November. For further information on dates and admission fees, contact:

Gaming and Wagering Business
7 Penn Plaza
New York, NY 10001-3900
Phone: 212-594-4120
Fax: 212-714-0514

4

Chips, Cards, Dice, and Other Gaming Devices

Most people don't think much one way or the other about poker chips, dice, or playing cards, but these items are extremely important parts of the casino industry.

Circus Circus Casino, Mississippi

CHIPS

What were once known as mere poker chips have taken on an entirely new identity over and beyond their original purpose. The new specially designed, high-tech chips serve as "casino currency." The tokens used by most casinos are usually unbreakable ten-gram clay, available in smooth or linen-texture surface, with designer graphics on both face and edge, and are completely washable. In addition, many chips are security coded with invisible ultraviolet markings which activate an alarm if taken into an unauthorized area. These chips, now bright and colorful and emblazoned with a particular casino's logo, have become highly collectible items in their own right. In fact, some casinos have paid for their full rack of chips in a matter of weeks, simply due to customers' keeping the chips as souvenirs rather than cashing them in.

At every casino, security is always a matter of top priority. Cash management, transfer, and storage can be major problems for any casino, especially considering the volume at which most operate. The possibility of counterfeiting is always present, even with poker chips and tokens. To reduce the possibility of this type of loss, as well as to count, sort, and assist in settlement of accounts, machines have been created which can greatly expedite these functions.

One such machine is the Chipco Pro-Sorter. Not only does this machine count and validate every chip, but it sorts the chips according to denomination. The machine is also fully integrated to most casino management software and hardware programs and can provide immediate on-line status reports, as well as automated output readings for state or federal regulatory reporting requirements. A similar machine, manufactured by the same company, is the Pro-Tech Cashier. This machine serves as a sort of automated teller machine. The player places his or her chips into a tray at the top of the machine. A scanner reads, validates, counts, and sorts the chips. The chips then remain in a holding box behind a clear plate of glass as the machine displays an exact dollar amount. If the player agrees with the amount displayed, he or she pushes a button and receives money. If the player disagrees with the machine's count or changes his or her mind, the player pushes a different button and his chips are immediately returned. Machines like these reduce cashier lines, improve player service, and catch counterfeit chips. In addition to casino use, chips are now used for keychains, business cards, drink tokens, and entertainment tickets, as well as for promotions and special events.

DICE

Dice are another interesting item. Few players ever stop to notice the dice upon which they place wagers. The first thing you will notice when looking closely at the dice used in casinos is that they are larger than dice used in home games. They are also translucent, that is, you can see through them but not clearly. Most casino dice are made from a colored cellulose acetate material which is formulated to provide the ultimate in clarity, hardness, and dimensional stability. Casino dice are made to precision tolerances of 1/10,000th of an inch, in other words, precise to within 1/20th the thickness of a human hair. All dice go through a lengthy and painstaking construction and finishing process. The cubes of cellulose acetate are cut a bit larger than the actual finished product. They are then drilled for precise placement of spots. The spots are filled in with a white resin for color. The excess coloring is then removed by a process known as a diamond or finish cut. The dice at this point are visually inspected for obvious blemishes or imperfections. If they pass this inspection, they are monogramed with the customer's logo. They are then "scalped" by hand, a process which removes the extra material which was displaced by the imprint of the casino's logo. The dice then pass through a three-stage "lapping" process during which they are trued and receive their final finish, either a smooth micropolished or satin finish, depending on the customer's preference. The dice are then rinsed, visually inspected for the last time, wrapped, boxed, and shipped.

Dice are replaced by casinos no less frequently than every eight hours, and sometimes more often than that. A pit boss will always take the dice when he or she leaves and brings new dice with him or her to the table. This lessens the chance that somebody can slip some loaded dice into the game. A pit boss may also change dice if a customer is winning too much, or if a player suspiciously throws the dice off the table. Security is important in all areas of casino activity, and dice are monitored like everything else.

CARDS

Playing cards, while not as complex as dice or chips, are also made to the highest possible quality control standards. Cards are either paper or plastic-coated paper, and are printed on both sides of a single sheet of paper, with one deck per sheet. The cards are then cut, boxed, wrapped, and shipped. The playing cards used by casinos are designed so that it would be very difficult to mark them in such a way that they could be used improperly. Like dice, playing cards are regularly replaced by casinos, especially if a gambler is having a strong run of good luck.

ROULETTE

Another gaming device to be found at all casinos is the ever popular roulette wheel. While the wheel has remained virtually unchanged for the last two hundred years, the materials with which it is constructed have been modified with time, as have the methods of manufacture. The first wheels were wooden, and many still are, but the majority are now made from machine-tooled ebonite, the same substance from which bowling balls are constructed. The use of precision machining, ebonite, aluminum, and high-tech plastics provides the finished product with a precision, balance, and durability which would have been unimaginable in the past.

TABLES

Another thing which the enthusiast will quickly notice is the brightly colored layouts on the individual gaming tables. While traditionally green in color, these felt layouts are becoming more colorful with the passage of time, the greens yielding to various shades of blue, red, and black. Every table layout is custom-designed and printed to order for each casino, from either plain or rubber-backed felt. The layouts are then affixed to the specific table for which they were intended, whether blackjack, roulette, craps, baccarat, poker, or other custom-designed house-specialty table games. The finished product is brightly colored, inviting, and pleasing to the eye.

SLOTS

While some games have not changed much over the centuries, most of the gaming devices have. These changes, in most cases, are the result of increased technical knowledge and ability on the part of the various manufacturers. The traditional "one-Armed bandit" has long been the favorite machine of the amateur gaming enthusiast. There are many reasons for this, but the single most likely reason is that the slot machine allows players the opportunity to play at any level they choose. This is as true in the riverboat casinos as on the land-based casinos, with slots accepting anything from a nickel to, in some cases, tokens worth thousands of dollars.

Slot machines have changed, though. While the traditional lever-operated slot machine still exists, it is no longer mechanical but is now totally electronic. A tug on the lever will not engage a series of gears, weights, and pullies, but instead will send a pulse of electrical energy through a series of circuits and transistors, resulting in a colorful graphic display on an illuminated screen. The traditional three-of-a-kind machines still exist, but they have been edged out by other, more diverse electronic video games, which offer a wide variety of games at one gaming position. Most of these new video games are operated by touchscreens or panel command buttons located on top or at the front of the machines. These machines are extremely sophisticated technically and feature such things as bill validators, which can check bills in every direction and in all denominations (except two-dollar bills). Other on-board features include progressive meters, high-speed graphics processors, battery-powered backup memory, multicolored LED displays, player-selectable games, adjustable pay tables, exciting sound effects, magnetic card readers for credit cards, and a player-selectable option for coin or credit play. These machines are in use today at all riverboat casinos and represent the state of the art in electronic gaming. Size and weight of the individual machines vary according to the type of machine in question. A standard conventional one-armed slot machine weighs in the neighborhood of 170 pounds. Some of the in-bar poker machines weigh approximately the same, while other single-player console units can weigh as much as 300 pounds.

Whatever the visitor to the riverboat casino chooses, whether traditional table games or the latest in electronic video games, the player is certain to be entertained with the best products and technology available today.

PART II

ROLL 'EM ON THE RIVER: THE RIVERBOAT GAMBLING SCENE

5

The Mississippi Boats

A t present, tourism is Mississippi's third-largest industry, after agriculture and manufacturing, and is directly responsible for in excess of 45,000 jobs. In addition to the jobs and income production of $1.7 billion, the state, county, and city taxes equal $192 million. The new riverboat and floating casinos in Mississippi are almost unbelievable in terms of their social and economic impact.

Mississippi has the most liberal riverboat gambling laws of all the states. There are no limits on bets or losses. Boats of any kind and design are permitted, from sidewheelers to sternwheel-

Ameristar, Vicksburg, Mississippi

ers to barges. Boats are not required to be in motion while gambling is underway, so casino owners do not have to bear the expense of making a boat seaworthy. The only areas of Mississippi in which riverboat gambling (or any other casino action) is permitted are in counties along the Mississippi River and along the Gulf coast. Before gambling can be approved, a referendum must be held in each county.

While other states such as Illinois, Missouri, and Louisiana have limited the number of casino licenses, this is not the case in Mississippi. As of this writing, there are, according to the Mississippi Gaming Commission, 120 applications for casino licenses on file. While some of them will withdraw and others will be denied by the state, nobody knows what the long-term effects of having so many casinos will be. The number will probably be limited at some point.

They say that the Mississippi Delta begins in the lobby of the Peabody Hotel in Memphis, Tennessee, and proceeds south from there. If so, the first real stop is Tunica, Mississippi, thirty or so miles south. Tunica is, or should I say, was, a small Southern town, something from a William Faulkner novel or a Tennessee Williams play. Nice houses situated on shady streets are surrounded by shacks on the edge of town, in an area often referred to as the poorest county in the richest country in the world. Driving south from Memphis down Highway 61, the traveler notices how rapidly the scenery changes, both geographically and socially. Small shacks, grain elevators, and flat land are about all there is to see. About midway between Memphis and Tunica is Walls, Mississippi, a smaller town than Tunica, known as the home of the Sacred Heart Auto League. Looking to the right, one notices an ever present high bank of land. This is the levy, a large manmade land bank, the only thing that stands between the unpredictable Mississippi River and the land. It is on the other side of the levy that the riverboats will be found.

The law in Mississippi mandates that riverboats must be permanently docked, that is, they are prohibited by law from leaving the dock for the purpose of conducting gaming activities with passengers aboard. This law would seem to defeat the purpose of riverboat gambling altogether, in the sense of riverboats as watergoing vessels. From the standpoint of the casino boat owners, however, this law is a big plus. By staying dockside, Mississippi boat owners save the high costs associated with operating a large boat. There are no engines, fuel, radar, or navigating equipment to buy, maintain, or operate. The savings resulting from these laws is incredible. And yet, even as much money as this saves the casino owners, it is nothing compared to the fact that as a result of being dockside and open twenty-four hours a day, there is a constant flow of customers. This is also a boon to the state of Mississippi, which takes 12 percent of the gross earnings brought in by the casinos.

The question naturally arises, Why not just build land-based casinos to begin with, rather than making somebody go to the trouble and pretense of building a riverboat which can't go anywhere? I wondered about this myself, especially after touring some of the riverboat construction sites and seeing how the boats were actually being built. A native of Tunica explained the reasoning to me. According to him, most of the population in Mississippi is against gambling of any kind, on moral and religious grounds. This, he explained, was due to the Magnolia State's location in the middle of the Bible Belt.

At the same time, Mississippi has had a poor economy for a long time. With little industry and commerce, and not much hope for change, there was a strong move afoot to bring in some jobs and revenue. The casinos would fill the bill nicely. Mississippi could allow boats on the Mississippi River and on the Gulf coast, and these operations would benefit from the large population bases centered in Memphis, to the north, and New Orleans, to the South.

With this in mind, legislation was passed which permitted only riverboat gambling, including river or Gulf cities, such as Clarksdale, Greenville, Vicksburg, and Natchez to the south, as well as Gulfport and Biloxi on the Gulf coast. By confining gambling to these waterfront areas, the rest of Mississippi geographically would be assured of never having to worry about land-based casinos in their backyards and yet at the same time would benefit from the improved overall economy of the state. There were still objections, but in the end, riverboat gambling legislation was passed in the state of Mississippi.

One question remains. Why aren't the riverboats actually running the river? It was decidedly to the casinos' advantage, as mentioned above, that they be permanently moored. This also serves the state well, since the more money the casinos take in, the more money the state takes in. Also, it is much cheaper to build floating casinos because they are more or less temporary structures they do not require as much or as expensive materials. According to C. J. Lawrence, the average cost of building a floating casino is generally between $10 million and $30 million, while land-based casinos, which are much larger than floating casinos, can often cost ten times that amount. In addition, the Mississippi River is still widely used as a highway for the transportation of freight and, to a lesser extent, of passengers. By keeping the gambling boats fixed in one place, many navigational problems which would have occurred have been eliminated at the outset.

In the early fall of 1993, I was given a tour of several riverboat sites, including Splash and Lady Luck in Tunica, and other sites to the north in Robinsonville, which were still under construction. What I saw was incredible and far beyond anything I would have ever imagined. In the first place, I expected to see boats sitting at docks on the banks of the Mississippi River. I assumed that these boats were actual riverboats and that they were seaworthy. Instead, what I found were not boats at all, but standard grain and oil barges which had been literally pulled out of the river and laid up on the land in predug pits.

I was shocked to say the least. These so-called riverboats were nothing more than barges, and as such, lacked engines, paddlewheels, propellers, or anything else which would enable them to move at all under their own power. After the barges were hauled out of the river and positioned in these ponds, they were then stripped of any superstructure, pipes, or other protruding materials by welders with torches. The ponds were then filled with water.

In most cases there were at least two barges that were joined together at the sides with welded steel braces. Upon these two flat barges, a superstructure several stories high was affixed which would eventually house the actual casino. Sitting on the ground off to either side of the floating casinos, and attached to them by walkways, support structures such as restaurants and gift shops were being built. Since the restaurants, music theaters, showrooms, and gift shops are not subject to the same rules as the actual casinos, they do not have to be in the water. Consequently, all of the space available for gambling is used for that purpose, with a minimum of wasted, that is, non-income-producing, space.

While the Tunica riverboats are not boats at all, per se, they are excellent casinos and are exquisitely decorated. Most of them have adopted a particular theme which is carried throughout everything associated with the casino, from decor, to food, to the costumes of the dealers and staff. The Treasure Bay Casino, for example, resembles a large pirate ship, while Fitzgeralds has the atmosphere of an Irish castle, and Harrah's looks like a floating plantation. Much time, effort, and expense have been invested in making each one unique and interesting. Patrons will not be disappointed.

The boats to the south are riverboats in a different sense than the ones in Tunica County. Some of them, like the Copa, located in Gulfport, are actually ships which have been converted to casino use. Others were ferrys, passenger boats, and other vessels, as well as some barges. Unlike the Tunica boats, however, some of these boats do not sit in ponds but are dockside and sit in the river. Like the Tunica boats, however, they do not ply the river but remain moored.

As we looked around the Tunica sites, I was amazed by the activity. Giant earthmoving machines moved rapidly from place to place, digging up dirt, pulling logs, and moving building materials. As far as the eye could see, construction was underway. I wondered how all of this would ever be put in place and in operation. My guide, a native of the area, asked my opinion. I was speechless. Earlier in the day, we had been talking about some of the very large species of poisonous snakes which call the area home, mainly for the benefit of an uninitiated casino operator from Detroit, via Las Vegas. As my guide had related his stories at the lunch table, I had watched the casino operator turn pale. As the three of us stood there now, at Tunica County's Robinsonville sight, a large poisonous cottonmouth crossed right in front of our big truck, undaunted by either our size or our presence.

TUNICA COUNTY

Tunica County, Mississippi, where riverboat gambling is permitted, is the riverfront county that is closest to Tennessee, and Memphis in particular. From the Tennessee border south to the city of Tunica, there are several different riverboat casino sites. Heading south on Highway 61, the first riverboat sites one finds are located in the area known as Robinsonville. This section of Tunica County includes the areas of Buck Lake, Buck Island, Polk's Landing, and Commerce Landing. Located at Buck Lake, closest to Memphis, is Grand Casino. Farther south you will find Binion's Horseshoe, the Circus Circus, and the Sheraton River Club Casino. Fitzgeralds is located at Polk's Landing. Still farther south there is Treasure Bay Casino. Even farther south is the area known as Commerce Landing. Harrah's, Sam's Town, The Summit, and the Southern Belle are located at this site. Farther south, but still north of Tunica, plans are scheduled for the Old River Casino Resort. The Mississippi Rose, while technically in Tunica, is actually on the Arkansas side of the Mississippi River. Sound confusing? It gets worse. At Mhoon Landing, in Tunica, are Splash, Lady Luck, Bally's, the President, the Copper Belle, the Jubilee Belle, and Lark's Landing Casino, which might be renamed by the time it is completed.

To simplify matters, here is a list of the casinos basically from north to south.

Buck Lake
Grand Casino

Farther South
Binion's Horseshoe
Circus Circus
Sheraton River Club Casino

Polk's Landing
Fitzgeralds

Treasure Bay (not at Polk's Landing, but the next boat
heading south)

Commerce Landing

Harrah's

Sam's Town

Southern Belle

Mhoon Landing

Bally's

Lady Luck

President Splash

Note: The reader is strongly urged to call in advance if there
are specific casinos on the gaming itinerary. While every effort
has been made to insure that the information provided here is
up-to-date and correct, it should be understood that the casino
market in Mississippi is in a constant state of flux and consequently subject to change without notice. There are over 120
casino applications on file at the Mississippi Gaming Commission. Since all of the operating casinos have toll-free numbers, a
quick call is worth the trouble.

Note: Because of the surplus of casinos in the Tunica, Mississippi, area—especially southern Tunica—traffic is a major problem. Many casinos have moved to become more accessible. President is scheduled to move to Davenport, Iowa, and Lady Luck has
moved from Mhoon Landing to Cahoma County. A new Lady Luck
is in the works for Northern Tunica County, closer to Memphis.

BUCK LAKE

Grand Casino

Grand Casinos, Inc., which also operates boats in Gulfport and
Biloxi, signed an agreement with Gaming Corporation of America
resulting in the purchase of a one-thousand-acre tract in northern Tunica County at Buck Lake, an oxbow lake of the Mississippi River. Grand Casinos, Inc., develops and manages casino
gaming facilities for Native American tribes on Native American
land, as well as its other properties. The company's common

stock is traded on the NASDAQ National Market System under the name GRND. Gaming Corporation of America is a public company specializing in the development of gaming markets. This joint project between the two companies is expected to be very successful due to its northernmost position in Tunica County.

Note: At the time of this writing, construction on Grand Casinos' Tunica County property has not yet started, but it is expected to be up and running by the end of 1994.

The Horseshoe Casino and Hotel

The Horseshoe Casino and Hotel, which opened in September 1994 is a gaming hotel, restaurant, and entertainment center located at the Casino Center in Robinsonville, in north Tunica County, Mississippi. The Casino Center property is a 220-acre development that includes over 4,000 parking spaces. Because of its close proximity to Memphis, the Casino Center is one of the most desirable of all casino locations in Mississippi. The original Horseshoe Hotel and Casino was founded in Las Vegas in 1951. In 1957, the Binion family became the sole owners and operators. The new Tunica County casino will follow in the same tradition, and will eventually employ 1,200 people.

As with most casinos, excess is the norm, and the Horseshoe is no exception. The luxurious three-story, 162,000-square-foot facility follows a late-Victorian-era San Francisco theme and will ultimately cost more than $72 million.

The casino itself, offers over 30,000 square feet of actual gaming space on one level, with 1,100 slot, video poker, and video keno games, and 48 table games, including blackjack, craps, roulette, poker, Caribbean stud, and big six.

A hotel is located on the second and third levels of the facility and continues the Victorian theme with 200 comfortably appointed guest rooms. Many of the hotel rooms overlook the courtyard and the only swimming pool currently available at any casino in Tunica County.

Club:	Name for club not yet decided
Admission:	No admission charge
Hours:	24 hours a day

Location: Casino Center Drive
Robinsonville, MS 38671

Phone: 1-800-303-7463

Sheraton Casino

The ITT Sheraton opened in August 1994, but at the time of this writing not much information was available. The casino features 1,000 slots as well as the standard array of table games, such as blackjack and various types of poker. The English Tudor theme of this casino is reflected in the exterior decor and carries through in interior appointments as well. The Sheraton is located at the Casino Center complex in the northern part of Tunica County, within walking distance of Circus Circus and the Horseshoe.

Location: 1 Casino Center Drive
Robinsonville, MS 38664

Phone: 601-363-4900 (A toll-free number has not yet been assigned)

Circus Circus

Circus Circus is a famous name in the Casino world of Nevada, with exotic casinos in Laughlin, Reno, and Las Vegas. The company started out in 1968 with the opening of Circus Circus on the Las Vegas strip. The Reno Circus Circus followed in 1978. The growth of the company has been measured and constant, with new properties added on a regular basis. Circus Circus went public in 1983 and is traded on the NYSE as PSE. It is the largest pure gaming company in the world and the largest employer in Nevada. The entry of this respected name into the casino arena of northern Mississippi promises to eventually rival its Luxor and Excalibur properties. Located in the Casino Center complex, along with the Sheraton and Horseshoe casinos, it is less than twelve miles from the Tennessee state line. The casino itself is housed in an 83,000-square-foot circus tent and offers over 60,000 square feet of gaming space, with 1,451 slot machines, 41 blackjack tables, 8 craps tables, 3 Caribbean stud tables, 10 poker tables, and 4 roulette wheels. The facility, which opened on

August 29, 1994, houses three restaurants, four bars, and strolling entertainment, ranging from circus acts to acrobats, a juggling stilt walker, and magicians.

Restaurant facilities include the Amazing Linguini Brothers, a fine Italian eatery seating 188, offering culinary specialties such as veal piccata and seafood pesto. Hours are from 5:00 P.M. until 10:30 P.M..

Jo Jo's Side Show Deli offers traditional deli sandwiches, as well as speciality sandwiches. It is open 24 hours, and also features a variety of pastries.

The Big Top Buffet, an 11,000-square-foot buffet features an international theme with dishes ranging from Mexican to Chinese. Hours are from 11:00 A.M. until 10:00 P.M..

Club:	Center Ring Club
Admission:	No admission charge
Hours:	24 hours a day
Location:	11 Casino Center Drive Robinsonville, MS 38664
Phone:	601-357-1111 (A toll-free number has not yet been assigned)

FARTHER SOUTH

Binion's Horseshoe, Circus Circus, and Sheraton River Club Casino

These three Farther South Casinos are now in position and located within walking distance of one another at an area known as Casino Center.

POLK'S LANDING

Fitzgeralds

Fitzgeralds is owned by the same company that operates Fitzgeralds casinos in Reno and Las Vegas. The 35,000-square-foot, two-story casino was built on two 260-by-50-foot barges by Yates Construction, and maintains an Irish theme throughout. The exterior appearance of the casino, which opened May 1, 1994, is that of an Irish castle. In fact, the casino's motto is "The Luck of the Irish Comes to Mississippi." Fitzgeralds has 1,060 slots and 54 table games and offers the gaming enthusiast a unique experience.

Fitzgeralds has two restaurants on the second level of the casino. Molly's is a 240-seat restaurant featuring full menu service and a buffet. The other restaurant, the Shamrock Express, offers good food for those who are short on time.

Also featured at this casino is a Card Club which consists of two cards: one for tables, and one for slots. Players using cards while they play earn bonus points good for meals, merchandise, and so on. The Card Club is similar to other slot clubs, which are described throughout the book.

Club:	Fitzgeralds Card Club
Admission:	No admission charge
Hours:	24 hours a day, 365 days a year
Location:	Commerce Landing Tunica, MS 38676
Phone:	1-800-766-LUCK

Treasure Bay

Treasure Bay, which opened on April 19, 1994, is probably the most interesting casino in Mississippi. This gigantic 400-foot-long, three-story floating casino was designed and built to resemble a pirate ship. Nothing has been left to the imagination outside or inside. The massive casino was constructed on four barges and has a steel mainmast which is 5 feet in diameter and nearly 300 feet tall. The interior continues the nautical theme throughout the 65,000-square-foot casino. With 1,680 slot and video machines and 62 table games, Treasure Bay is, in terms of gaming positions, one of the largest floating casinos in America.

Club:	Treasure Seekers, a slot club.
Admission:	No admission charge

Hours: 24 hours a day, 365 days a year
Location: 1 Treasure Bay Drive
              Robinsonville, MS 38664
Phone: 1-800-727-7684

COMMERCE LANDING

Harrah's

Harrah's was founded by the legendary Bill Harrah in Reno, Nevada, in 1937 as a bingo parlor. A Lake Tahoe operation opened in 1955. Holiday Inns, Inc., acquired the company in 1980. In 1990 Harrah's became the gaming subsidiary of the Promus Companies (listed on the New York, Midwest, Pacific, and Philadelphia stock exchange using ticker symbol PRI). As a company, Harrah's employs over 23,000 persons nationwide and operates hotel/casinos in Atlantic City, Lake Tahoe, Reno, Laughlin, and Las Vegas. In addition to the above, Harrah's now operates casinos in Joliet, Illinois, and Tunica and Vicksburg, Mississippi. Other companies under the Promus banner include Embassy Suites, Homewood Suites, and Hampton Inns. All told, Harrah's owns and operates 601 game tables, 11,541 slot machines, and has a total casino space of 435,566 square feet. The mission at Harrah's is "to be the world's premier company in casino entertainment, with the best people creating a great time for every customer, every time, guaranteed." Judging from their position in the casino world, their mission is being accomplished daily.

The Harrah's property in Tunica is a plantation-themed design, which includes 32,000 square feet of actual casino space, with 54 game tables, 1,203 slot machines, and a nonsmoking area on the second deck. The 30,000-square-foot shoreside facilities include a coffee shop, buffet, gift shop, and parking for 1,300 cars.

Club: Harrah's Gold Card
Admission: No admission charge
Hours: 24 hours a day, 365 days a year
Location: Commerce Landing–Robinsonville Rd.
              Robinsonville, MS 38664
Phone: 1-800-HARRAH'S

Sam's Town Hotel and Gambling Hall

Sam's Town, which opened in spring 1994, claims to be the largest hotel/casino complex in the state of Mississippi. The western-themed complex is owned by the Boyd Gaming Corporation, a Nevada-based public company, which is traded on the New York Stock Exchange under the name BOYDGM N. The gigantic complex includes a 200-room hotel, a 1,500-seat concern and theater facility, and 92,000 square feet of actual casino space.

Club:	Yes; call for information
Admission:	No admission charge
Hours:	24 hours a day, 365 days a year
Location:	Robinsonville Rd.
	Robinsonville, MS 38664
Phone:	1-800-456-0711

Southern Belle

The Southern Belle, which opened in January 1993, is located twenty miles south of Memphis in the Commerce Road area known as "Riverbend." The three-story, 150,000-square-foot Southern Belle is designed after a traditional plantation and features famous Southern hospitality in a warm and elegant setting. The Southern Belle was started by Mississippi Riverboat Amusements, Ltd., owner of the Biloxi Belle in Biloxi, Mississippi. At the time of this writing, the company has reorganized as a first step in going public. The new company will be known as Belle Casinos, Inc. The Tunica casino offers more than 60,000 square feet of actual gaming space, with 1,300 slot machines, 75 table games, and a special poker area. The Belle's second and third decks are the setting for fine dining, great entertainment, and retail shops. The restaurant facilities include a gourmet dining room as well as the 500-seat Delect-a-belle Buffet, for casual dining. While work progressed on the casino, a training shop was established in nearby Walls, Mississippi, where dealer trainees learned their skills.

Club:	Call for information
Admission:	No admission charge
Hours:	24 hours a day, 365 days a year

Location: (Off U.S. 55, exit at Hernando, west on
               Miss. 304 for 30 miles)
               Tunica, MS 38676
  Phone: 601-363-4242

MHOON LANDING

Bally's

Bally's Saloon and Gambling Hall is a twenty-acre complex featuring a western-themed dockside casino, a saloon, and a land-
based restaurant area. The casino, with 45,000 square feet of
actual gaming space, is owned by Bally Manufacturing Company
in Chicago, and claims to be the largest casino in Tunica. The $40
million project was built by the Roy Anderson Corporation of
Gulfport, Mississippi, and contains 1,150 state-of-the-art slot
machines, playing denominations from 25¢ to $25.00. In addition
to this large number of slots, there are also 13 progressive slot
links which offer players the opportunity to win constantly
increasing jackpots, including the Mississippi-based Megabucks,
which starts at $1 million. There are a total of 65 game tables,
with 41 blackjack, 4 roulette, 8 craps, 8 poker, 2 mini-baccarat, 1
Big Six, and 1 Red Dog.

The 4,000-square-foot Saloon is adjacent to the casino and features a number of interesting things to do. From nightly country
music concerts, to dance lessons, to karaoke, the Saloon has
something for everyone. In addition to the above, there is a giant-
screen television in the bar for sporting events. The Saloon is
open daily from 2:00 P.M. until 3:00 A.M., and there is no cover
charge.

Bally's is also noted for having brought the first McDonald's
restaurant to Tunica. While this might seem like a dubious dis-
tinction to some, the McDonald's Food Court at Bally's is like no
McDonald's you've ever seen before, and offers 20,000 square feet
of great food, including everything from gourmet pizza and Oscar
Meyer hot dogs, to Breyer's ice cream and Entenmann's pastries.

In addition to the Tunica property, Bally's also operates Bally's
Park Place and the Grand Casino Resorts in Atlantic City, New
Jersey, and Bally's Las Vegas Casino Resort in Nevada.

Club: Bally's was one of the pioneers in the gaming club area and in Tunica has the Bally's Gold Star Club. All slot machines in the casino accept the Gold Star Club card. Membership is free, and players qualify for merchandise and other club member benefits.

Admission: No admission charge

Hours: 24 hours a day, 7 days a week

Location: Mhoon Landing
Tunica, MS 38676

Phone: 1-800-382-2559

Lady Luck

Lady Luck Gaming Corporation is a Las Vegas–based operation "dedicated to providing a quality entertainment product for our customers; to be a productive member of the community; and to strengthen through prosperity our shareholders' investment." The philosophy seems to be working, since Lady Luck Gaming Corporation is one of the fastest-growing casino management companies in the country. What started in 1963 as a privately owned newsstand in downtown Las Vegas has developed into a major player in the high-stakes riverboat game. The Lady Luck Hotel Casino in downtown Las Vegas is one of downtown's major attractions. In addition to the property in Las Vegas, and another in Central City, Colorado, there are the Lady Luck riverboat casinos in Tunica, Cahoma County, Vicksburg, Natchez, Gulfport, Biloxi, Mississippi, and the Lady Luck Kimmswick in Jefferson County, Missouri, 120 miles from Little Rock, Arkansas.

Lady Luck went public in 1993 and raised a quick $22 million in an initial stock offering. The original stock offering consisted of 4,500,000 common shares at $16.00 per share. Prior to this the company had privately raised approximately $37 million through the sale of first mortgage bonds.

The Las Vegas–themed Lady Luck casino formerly in Mhoon Landing is now located immediately south of Tunica in Cahoma County, Mississippi and is now known as the Lady Luck Rhythm and Blues. With 665 slots and 44 gaming tables. The floating casino was constructed upon two linked barges, with one barge offering 25,000 square feet of gaming area. The second barge consists of a restaurant, coffee shop, buffet, and snack bar. For entertainment, Lady Luck offers an outdoor laser light show. It was the second casino to open in the Tunica area. With around-the-clock casino action and unlimited betting, Lady Luck is perfect for the serious gaming enthusiast. In addition to the slots and gaming tables, the casino features a tickets sports bar and two excellent restaurants. Considering the commitment of Lady Luck to the growing riverboat market, it is safe to say that Lady Luck casinos are likely to control a large share of the market.

Club:	Mad Money; call for information
Admission:	No admission charge
Hours:	24 hours a day, 365 days a year
Location:	777 Lady Luck Parkway Lula, MS 38644
Phone:	1-800-789-LUCK

President

The President Casino in Tunica is a joint venture between President Riverboat Casinos and Jackpot, Inc. The 2,000-person-capacity riverboat casino, which is located next to Lady Luck, opened in December 1993 and is the sister ship of the President in Biloxi. The conversion to casino configuration was handled by Leevac Shipyards in Jennings, Louisiana, one of the major builders in the riverboat business. The 292-by-65-foot President is an authentic traditional sternwheeler with 700 slot and video games, 41 tables, and over 25,000 square feet of actual casino space.

Food services include Dale's Deli and Dale's Buffet.

Club:	Jackpot Slot Club
Admission:	No admission charge
Hours:	24 hours a day, 365 days a year
Location:	Mhoon Landing Tunica, MS 38676
Phone:	1-800-WIN-2121

(At press time, the President Casino at Mhoon Landing is closed for several months and is scheduled to move to Davenport, IA, at some point in the future.)

Splash

Located at Mhoon Landing in Tunica, Splash, with 650 slots, 22 blackjack tables, and 9 poker tables, was the first riverboat casino to open in Tunica County (in August 1992). As the first, it took quick advantage of being the one and only. As a result of this status, it was able to charge a $10 admission fee, and continued this policy until late 1993, by which time Lady Luck, Harrah's, and Bally's had opened. Charging an entrance fee just to get in the place was considered greedy, excessive, and unnecessary by many of the local residents who took offense and vowed to boycot Splash as soon as any other casino opened. The casino, on the other hand, felt that the admission price would dissuade the idle curiosity seekers from interfering with those who were there to gamble. The fee might have irritated the public, but not to the extent that any large numbers stayed away. In fact, there were so many people waiting to get in that Splash had to erect a large tent to hold them all for the duration of the wait, which, I am told, lasted in some cases for several hours. Be that as it may, the admission fee was reported to have gained the casino an additional $10 million during the period in which it was in effect.

Club:	Splash Cash Club; call for information
Admission:	No admission charge (was $10)
Hours:	24 hours a day, 365 days a year
Location:	Splash Casino
	Mhoon Landing
	Tunica, MS 38676
Phone:	1-800-344-DICE

Tunica County Chamber of Commerce

The Tunica County Chamber of Commerce had been closed for a while before the riverboat casino boom, due to lack of business. It is again alive and well and doing business. Phone: 601-363-2865

CLARKSDALE

Lady Luck Rhythm & Blues

For over a year the residents of Cahoma County watched the riverboat money roll into neighboring Tunica County to the north. On August 24, 1993, they voted to allow riverboat casinos. The first one on line, which opened in 1994, is Lady Luck, which also operates the Lady Luck in Natchez. A 30,000-square-foot dockside facility is planned to adjoin the 18,000-square-foot casino.

Location:	(On the Mississippi side of the Helena Bridge)
Phone:	1-800-789-LUCK

Clarksdale/Cahoma County Chamber of Commerce

Phone: 601-627-7337

GREENVILLE

Cotton Club

The Cotton Club is Greenville's first riverboat casino. This deluxe boat features blackjack, craps, Big 6, roulette, poker, video poker, Multiple Action 21, and plenty of slot machine action. Gourmet dining is featured at the Dockside Restaurant and Lounge. Free secured parking. Tour groups and RVs welcome. Must be 21 with valid ID to enter.

Club:	High Cotton Slot Club
Admission:	$10
Hours:	24 hours a day, 7 days a week
Location:	mailing address, PO Box 1777 (Where Main Street meets the river) Greenville, MS 38702
Phone:	1-800-WIN-MORE

Las Vegas Casino

The Las Vegas Casino in Greenville is owned by Casino Gaming International, a Nevada company based in Las Vegas. This project is particularly interesting in that the boat was constructed on site, using mostly local laborers and subcontractors. From the very outset the casino was welcomed by the citizens of Greenville, and the relationship between the casino owners and the town has continued to flourish. The facility now employs in excess of 600 persons. The casino itself was constructed upon a barge, as most of the Mississippi boats have been. The exterior features of the structure are not particularly remarkable, but the inside is very open and spacious, with 19-foot ceilings. The casino owners sought to accomplish two main objectives with the Las Vegas Casino, the first being to create an enviornment similar to Las Vegas casinos, one which is both comfortable and spacious. The casino owners also wanted to have something for everybody, and with this in mind, have slots starting at five cents. The casino has selected the motto "Biggest Little Casino in the World," and seems to have accomplished both objectives. The casino opened in March 1994.

The 18,000-square-foot casino has 515 slot machines, 4 craps tables, 20 blackjack tables, 2 roulette wheels, 10 keno machines, 1 Big Six wheel, and 6 poker tables in a special mezzanine area.

Club:	Wild Card; call for information
Admission:	No admission charge
Hours:	24 hours a day, 7 days a week
Location:	mailing address, PO Box 1294 (Downtown Greenville on the waterfront) Greenville, MS 38701
Phone:	1-800-Vegas-21

Greenville Chamber of Commerce

Phone: 601-378-3141.

VICKSBURG

Vicksburg, Mississippi, is one of the most interesting places around. First and foremost, the area is noted for its rich historical heritage. The Vicksburg National Military Park is one of the largest Civil War battlefield memorials in the country. From the giant cannon placed on high bluffs overlooking the river to the magnificent monuments placed on the battlefield by the states whose soldiers died there, the Vicksburg battlefield is most impressive. There is a visitor center and museum which contain artifacts and exhibits from the battle, as well as maps and diagrams. The visitors center is open daily.

Perhaps the most fascinating display at the battlefield is the Union ironclad *Cairo*, which was sunk by the proud soldiers of the Confederate States during the first northern invasion. It was the first ship in maritime history to have been destroyed by an electronically detonated device. For over one hundred years, the remains of this large steam-powered warship lay at the bottom of the river. Its original iron armor plates have been reconstructed around a wooden frame. The visitor is able to walk around and through the ironclad. It is an incredible sight.

The old courthouse, another wonderful attraction, contains one of the most interesting museums in America and features many historic items and some excellent examples of Confederate memorabilia.

> Vicksburg Convention and Visitors Bureau
> (Corner of Highway 27 and Clay St.)
> PO Box 1294
> Phone: 1-800-221-3536

Vicksburg-Warren County Chamber of Commerce

Phone: 601-636-1012

Ameristar

The Ameristar Casino, which was built by Yates Construction, claims to be the largest riverboat casino in Vicksburg. The mammoth casino was constructed on a double barge, and is 300 feet long by 120 feet wide, has three decks, and maintains a late Victorian theme throughout. The casino has 1,050 slot and video games as well as 68 gaming tables, featuring the standard games found in most casinos. The Ameristar has taken the lead in the entertainment field and is the first boat in the area to feature truly top name performers. The Ameristar's 350-seat showroom had scheduled, at the time of this writing, such major acts as Lou Rawls, Louise Mandrell, the Smothers Brothers, and Roy Clark.

The Ameristar property features the excellent land-based Delta Point Restaurant, long a Vicksburg landmark. The restaurant building is situated on the side of a hill overlooking the Mississippi River and provides an excellent and romantic view of the river, the casino, and the bridge. The Ameristar has three separate and unique restaurants on board. The Galley is a deli which is open for lunch and dinner. The Pilot House serves a breakfast, lunch, and dinner buffet, featuring a variety of American favorites. The Veranda is a casual family-style restaurant.

> *Club:* The Ameristar Casino has a players' club called the Ameristar Club which offers free membership. Call for details, or apply at the casino.
>
> *Admission:* No admission charge
>
> *Hours:* 24 hours a day, 365 days a year
>
> *Location:* 4111 Washington St. Vicksburg, MS 39181
>
> *Phone:* 1-800-700-7770

Harrah's

Harrah's Vicksburg riverboat was the first to enter the Vicksburg market, coming on line in the fall of 1993. The $49 million project has an actual casino floor space of 20,000 square feet, houses 600 slot machines and 48 game tables, and accommodates 1,200 passengers.

The dockside facility includes a 117-room Harrah's Hotel, a city park, and a greenbelt with a boardwalk along the city's waterline.

> *Club:* Call for information
>
> *Admission:* No admission charge
>
> *Hours:* 24 hours a day, 365 days a year

ate555

Location: 1310 Mulberry St.
            Vicksburg, MS 39180
Phone: 1-800-HARRAHS

Isle of Capri

The Isle of Capri opened on August 9, 1993, with 515 slots and 35 tables, but soon expanded to 640 slots and 45 table games. The Isle of Capri in Vicksburg originally opened using the Diamond Lady boat and the Lucky 7 pavilion. These were replaced by new facilities in May 1994.

Club: Island Gold
Admission: Free admission and parking
Hours: 24 hours a day
Location: 3990 Washington St.
            Vicksburg, MS 39180
Phone: 1-800-WIN-ISLE

Lady Luck (scheduled to open in the fall of 1994)

The Lady Luck in Vicksburg employs the traditional showboat theme and has an actual gaming area of 26,000 square feet. No address or opening date is yet available.

Location: (2 miles from downtown and directly
            South of I-20)
            Vicksburg, MS 39180
Phone: No number at this time

NATCHEZ

Lady Luck

Lady Luck, which opened in the spring of 1993, was the first riverboat to open in Natchez. The dockside casino was designed to resemble the historic Natchez-based *J. M. White* riverboat which used to travel the Mississippi in the late 1800s. The 25,000-square-foot dockside facility features 14,300 square feet of gam-

ing area, with 515 slots and 33 gaming tables. There is a lounge,
a bar, a gourmet restaurant, a buffet/coffee shop, and a gift shop.

Club:	Mad Money Club
Admission:	No admission charge
Hours:	24 hours a day
Location:	Lady Luck
	21 Silver St.
	Natchez, MS 39120
Phone:	1-800-722-5825

Natchez-Adams Chamber of Commerce

Phone: 601-445-4611

THE GULF COAST

The Mississippi Gulf Coast is the site of several important boats,
as outlined below. With an immediate local area population base
of 500,000, the Gulf Coast represents the second-largest population block in the state. In addition, the Gulf Coast is blessed with
beautiful beaches, a mild climate, and easy access by land, air,
and sea. The population base within one hundred miles in any
direction reaches in the millions. Biloxi, or example, is about 75
miles from New Orleans, 75 miles from Mobile, and 160 miles
from Jackson. It is currently estimated that visitors to the Gulf
Coast exceed 2 million annually. The casinos are expected to add
another million or more to that number each year.

BAY ST. LOUIS

Casino Magic

Casino Magic Corporation was incorporated on April 17, 1992, as
a Minnesota corporation and has five subsidiaries: Mardi Gras
Casino Corporation, Bay St. Louis Corporation, Biloxi Casino
Corporation, Gulfport Casino Corporation, and Atlantic/Pacific
Corporation. The common stock of Casino Magic is listed on the
NASDAQ National Market System under the symbol CMAG.

Casino Magic was one of the first organizations to obtain a gaming license in Mississippi, and started out with the intention of being the biggest and the best. Apparently the dream has been realized. Located forty miles from New Orleans on a sprawling 530-acre site on the back bay in Bay St. Louis, Casino Magic's property is the largest dockside casino development in the world. The 40,000-square-foot casino features 65 gaming tables, over 1,250 slots, and live keno. In addition to the 40,000 square feet of casino space, there is a 90,000-square-foot support facility which is up and running, as are a marina and RV park.

The RV park has over one hundred state-of-the-art sites now available. Each spot has full hook-up, including water, electricity, sewage, cable TV, barbeque grill, and picnic table. Shower and laundromat facilities are located on the grounds, which are located within easy walking distance of the casino complex. Shuttle to and from the casino complex is also available. The RV park is open twenty-four hours a day, seven days a week, and costs only $14.95 per day. Reservations are recommended and may be made by calling the casino's regular number, 1-800-5-MAGIC-5.

Development at the site is ongoing and is expected to continue for another six or seven years. A 1,500-room hotel and a full-service convention center opened in late 1994, as did a twenty-seven-hold golf course and an eighteen-hole putting green designed and managed by Arnold Palmer's company. Ultimately tennis courts, a children's arcade, a water park, and townhouses will become a part of the overall complex.

As a result of capacity crowds and an increased need for additional space, The 387-foot Dubuque Casino Belle, a 30,000-square-foot casino, was brought down from Iowa temporarily in 1993 to help accommodate crowds.

Travel service:	Casino Magic Vacations, located in Chicago, operates 85 flights a month from 45 cities, delivering passengers to Casino Magic properties in Bay St. Louis and Biloxi. Call for specific information.
Phone:	1-800-MAGIC-50

Club:	Players Club
Admission:	No admission charge
Hours:	24 hours, 365 days a year
Location:	711 Casino Magic Drive
	Bay St. Louis, MS 39520
Phone:	1-800-5-MAGIC-5

Hancock County Chamber of Commerce

Phone: 601-467-9048

GULFPORT

Copa Casino

The Copa, located in Gulfport, is one of my favorite dockside casinos. Formerly a cruise ship known as the *Pride of Mississippi*, the sleek ship is over 500 feet long and has been converted to a 30,000-square-foot casino with 721 slots and 45 game tables. The atmosphere at the Copa is tropical, casual, and comfortable and showcases the glamour and excitement of casino gaming in a world-class luxury setting. Interior design was handled by Val Thornton's Denver-based Design Concepts Studio. Custom-designed carpets, chandeliers, hand-wrought copper murals, and etched glass combine with extensive use of brass and hardwoods to create a lavish interior, all the more impressive due to its certification as a clean-air, smoke-free environment.

In addition to 383 quarter slots, 75 nickel slots, 237 $1 slots, 12 $5 slots, 3 $25 slots, blackjack, roulette, craps, baccarat, poker, and Big Six, there are other special promotions, including car giveaways, 99-cent lunch specials at the cafe on Mondays, Wednesdays, and Fridays, double pays on some slots at certain times, and other unannounced specials.

Restaurant facilities on the boat include the Copa Cabana Cafe, a deli-style restaurant, and Po Boys, which offers speciality sandwiches, soups, and salads. There are three on-board bars serving free cocktails for players. The Raintree Lounge provides free live entertainment on weekends.

As an example of what a riverboat can mean to an area financially, it is estimated that the Copa will contribute approximately $4.7 million in taxes to the state and $1.5 million to the city of Gulfport within any twelve-month period. The Copa Casino already employes more than 750 people with an annual payroll in excess of $10 million.

Docked next to the Copa is another boat, the Aegean Princess. This craft houses a great restaurant featuring smoked prime rib, fresh seafood, and salads. Weekday lunch specials are available, starting at $3.95. The Aegean Princess Restaurant is open Sunday through Thursday, 11:30 A.M. to midnight, and Friday and Saturday until 1:00 A.M..

Club:	There is no slot club as such at the time of this writing, but most likely there will be one soon. Call for information.
Admission:	No admission charge
Hours:	24 hours a day, 365 days a year
Location:	East Pier 52 Gulfport, MS
Phone:	1-800-WIN-COPA

Grand Casino

Opened on May 15, 1993, this 200,000-square-foot casino is billed as the world's largest floating casino. It was built by Service Marine Industries, Inc., in Morgan City, Louisiana. With over 90,000 square feet of gaming space, it is three stories tall and has over 1,800 slots, playing denominations from 5 cents to $100. There are 85 gaming tables, including blackjack, roulette, craps, baccarat, and Pai Gow poker. In addition, there is live keno, and a Poker Room featuring over 20 tables. The boat is a whopping 600 feet long, 111 feet wide, and 72 feet tall and has a total of 4,100 gaming positions. An additional 135,000 square feet serve as office and restaurant space. This $80 million project drew a record crowd of 35,000 patrons during its first two days of operation. A theater is under construction which will feature top-name country music stars.

Other Grand Casino features include a festive buffet featuring the Coast's finest cuisine, a variety of speciality restaurants, a supervised children's activity center, championship golf courses, convenient shopping, and clean, white sand beaches.

Club:	Grand Advantage Club
Admission:	No admission charge
Hours:	24 hours a day, 365 days a year
Location:	3215 West Beach Blvd. (Highway 90) Gulfport, MS 39501
Phone:	1-800-WIN-7777

Lady Luck (opening in the fall of 1994)

The Lady Luck in Gulfport is a Southern-theme dockside casino in the small-craft harbor of Gulfport. This 40,000-square-foot facility offers 28,000 square feet of gaming area, 650 slots, and 39 table games.

Location:	(At the intersection of Highway 90 and Interstate)
Phone:	Not yet available

Mississippi Gulf Coast Chamber of Commerce

Phone: 601-863-2933

BILOXI

Biloxi Belle

The Biloxi Belle Casino Resort opened on August 28, 1992, and is operated by Mississippi Riverboat Amusement, Ltd. The boat itself had originally been constructed as the 217-by-44-foot riverboat *Wayward Lady* but was converted to a casino configuration prior to opening in 1992. The casino, with 28,000 square feet of gaming space, was originally part of a large hotel/casino complex which operated in excess of 700 slots, 12 blackjack, and 8 poker tables. Business, however, was so incredible that the original operation was replaced in 1994 by a new three-story edifice set upon barges measuring 443 feet by 116 feet. The new $40.65 million property offers over 150,000 square feet of interior space, with 50,000 square feet of actual gaming space. The new casino features 1,200 slot machines and 75 gaming tables. Like its predecessor, it is open twenty-four hours a day, 365 days a year. A children's activity center has been established adjacent to the casino to provide supervised professional child care for gaming patrons. The children's center includes an indoor playground, game arcade, video entertainment, and a specially designed infant and toddler area.

The entire resort is styled to resemble an antebellum plantation, with the casino showcased as a Southern mansion. The grounds leading to the casino's columned portico include gardens, fountains, and inlaid brick walkways. The visitor to the new Biloxi Belle is greeted by wide sweeping staircases reminiscent of *Gone With the Wind*'s Tara. The elegance of the old South is reflected in the interior decor throughout the entire casino, including extensive use of stained woodwork, interior columns, and faux marble.

The first floor of this magnificent undertaking offers 40,000 square feet of gaming space, including a baccarat pit which is partially glass-enclosed and visible from both grand staircases as well as the second level. At the end of the first floor is a large stage for live entertainment.

The second level includes 10,000 square feet of gaming space, a twenty-four-hour coffee shop, a buffet, and a gourmet restaurant. The third floor houses the casino's administrative offices, as well as a 20,000-square-foot special events center with a seating capacity of 1,500.

Club:	Lucky Belle
Admission:	No admission charge
Hours:	24 hours a day, 365 days a year
Location:	857 Beach Blvd. (at the foot of I-110 and US 90) Biloxi, MS 39530
Phone:	1-800-BILOXI-7

Casino Magic

Phase one of Casino Magic opened June 5, 1993. Operations expanded and the second phase opened in October 1993. With 1,075 slots, 65 gaming tables, including blackjack tables and 14 poker tables, and a total space of over 115,000 square feet, Casino Magic's Biloxi site is one of the largest in the area. Restaurant facilities, including a buffet and fast food, are available dockside.

Travel Service:	Casino Magic Vacations, located in Chicago, operates 85 flights a month from 45 different cities, delivering passengers to Casino Magic's Bay St. Louis and Biloxi casinos. Call for information.
Phone:	1-800-MAGIC-50
Club:	Magic Money
Admission:	No admission charge
Hours:	24 hours a day, 365 days a year
Location:	167 Beach Blvd. Biloxi, MS 39535
Phone:	1-800-729-9257

Gold Shore Casino

The Gold Shore Casino is owned by American Gaming Corporation, a Mississippi company. The Biloxi property represents its first entry into the gaming business. A second property, the Gold River Casino, is in the planning stages for Vicksburg.

The Gold Shore, which opened in April 1994, was built on site in Biloxi with Tommy Herbert serving as the general contracting foreman. The barge is 330 feet by 110 feet, with a total of 109,000 square feet. The boat is three stories tall, with an exterior theme reminiscent of the New Orleans French Quarter. The boat's interior is Victorian, with rich colors and extensive brass trim. The casino itself has a total gaming area of 66,000 square feet, which includes 900 slot machines, 230 video poker machines, and 60 gaming tables. The second floor houses three food service areas, including a steak house, a buffet, and a snack bar.

The dockside facilities, situated in the old Gulf National Life building (known as the G & L site), contain a passenger holding area as well as general corporate offices and security services.

Club:	There is a players' club, and a senior citizens' club, both of which offer free membership. Call for information.
Admission:	No admission charge
Hours:	24 hours a day, 365 days a year
Location:	771 Beach Blvd. (Off Highway 90) Biloxi, MS 39530
Phone:	1-800-WIN-GOLD

Grand Casino

Grand Casino has established a strong gaming presence in Mississippi, beginning with the Gulfport site and continuing in Biloxi and Tunica. The Grand Casino in Biloxi represents the company's second property on the Gulf coast. Barges arrived in May 1993 and construction began immediately on the Las Vegas–style property. While the Grand Casino Biloxi falls under the legal category of a riverboat in the sense that it is a floating casino, that's where the similarity ends. Grand Casino Biloxi is a floating casino, but no attempt has been made to make it look like a riverboat. It resembles a Las Vegas casino with its modern, contemporary exterior. Interior appointments are reminiscent of an 1890s casino. No expense has been spared to make this casino the best possible. The Biloxi property is every bit as as large in scope as the Gulfport casino. In fact, the property is 250,000 square feet overall, with 100,000 square feet of actual casino space. In addition to the Casino, which boasts 1,800 slots and 100 table games, Grand Casino has built a theater with a capacity of almost 1,900. This theater features top-name country music stars and follows a similar format as the theaters in Branson, Missouri. Restaurant facilities include Sister's, for fine dining, and LB's Steak House, the Market Place Buffet, and Roxy's a fifties-style diner.

Club:	Grand Advantage Club
Admission:	No admission charge
Hours:	24 hours a day, 365 days a year
Location:	Highway 90 at Point Cadet Biloxi, MS 39530
Phone:	1-800-946-2946

Isle of Capri

The Isle of Capri, owned by Casino America, Inc., opened on August 1, 1992, and was the first gaming operation to open in Mississippi during modern times. The casino is situated within a 60,000-square-foot, multilevel gaming complex, featuring a floating pavilion and a 201-foot-long riverboat. The casino has 1,135 slots, including video poker and progressive slots, featuring Win-A-Car, Mississippi Nickels, Quartermania, and Megabucks, not to mention Mississippi's largest jackpot, starting at $1 million. There are a total of 50 gaming tables, featuring 36 blackjack, 6 craps, 1 Pai Gow poker, 1 mini-baccarat, 3 roulette, 1 Big Six wheel, and 5 Caribbean poker. In addition, there is a Poker Paradise Room featuring Seven-Card Stud, Texas Hold 'Em, and Omaha.

On June 23, 1993, a new floating pavilion opened, replacing the earlier barge with a two-level 50,000-square-foot complex. The new pavilion continues the casino's tropical theme with an animated parrot, 34 fiberglass palm trees, a 6,000-square-foot mirror, a neon wave wall, and a two-story waterfall with a rock stairway. A simulated thunderstorm with realistic sound and lighting effects activates every twenty minutes. The 317-by-74-foot facility was constructed entirely by Mississippi contractors at Ham Marine in Pascagoula, and McDermott & Company Shipyard in Gulfport.

Pavilion facilities include the 350-seat Calypso's Restaurant, featuring the best of local cuisine and house specialities twenty-four hours a day. Calypso's also features a 3,500-square-foot lounge enclosed by a two-level atrium. The lounge offers tropical drinks and live music fourteen hours a day. An in-house gift shop, the Banana Cabana, presents an interesting selection of gifts and souvenirs.

Club:	Island Gold Players Club
Admission:	No admission charge
Hours:	24 hours a day, 365 days a year
Location:	151 Beach Blvd.
	Biloxi, MS 39530
Phone:	1-800-THE-ISLE

Lady Luck

The Lady Luck Biloxi joins four existing casinos and another nine pending, at the Harrison County location off Highway 90, four miles south of Interstate 10. Located on a one-acre site on this prime property, Lady Luck establishes its presence with an Asian theme, including a huge fire-breathing dragon which emerges periodically from the water. The facility is over 45,000 square feet in size, with 25,000 square feet for gaming. The Lady Luck has 656 slots and video games accepting denominations from 25¢ to $25.00. There are 38 gaming tables featuring craps, blackjack, roulette, Carribbean stud poker, mini-baccarat, and other popular games. The Asian theme is unique to the Mississippi floating casinos and is well worth seeing.

Club:	Mad Money
Admission:	No admission charge
Hours:	24 hours a day, 365 days a year
Location:	Lady Luck Biloxi
	315 Beach Blvd. (U.S. 90 2 miles east of
	Biloxi Lighthouse)
	Biloxi, MS 39530
Phone:	1-800-539-LUCK

President Casino

President Riverboat Casinos operates properties in Biloxi and Tunica, Mississippi, as well as Davenport, Iowa, and St. Louis, Missouri, with other projects currently underway. As a company, its contributions to these cities and areas go far beyond the substantial revenues which the operations add to state and local coffers. In the Davenport area, for instance, the President Casino is the sixth-largest employer. In Biloxi the company has restored the historic Broadwater Hotel and contributed to the rejuvenation of the Gulf Coast. In Tunica the President Riverboat Casino has created jobs in an area where employment was previously almost nonexistent. In addition, President Riverboat Casinos is actively involved in charitable work and contributions in every locale in which it operates, and is widely considered to be a good neighbor. The President Riverboat Casino in Biloxi opened August 13, 1992. The craft is 292 feet long, 65 feet wide, has a passenger capacity of 2,000, and has 21,500 square feet of actual casino space. Built as a replica of a nineteenth-century sidewheeler by LeeVac Shipyard in Jennings, Louisiana, the boat features 620 slot machines and 49 table games. Among the table games are craps, blackjack, roulette, mini-baccarat, Caribbean Stud, Pai Gow poker, and a live poker parlor with 8 tables.

The three-story boat is permanently docked at the world-famous Broadwater Beach Resort, an 800-room hotel with tennis courts, two 18 hole golf courses, pools, and beach facilities.

The President Casino complex offers several excellent restaurants. The Broadwater Marina Features fresh seafood and Italian cuisine. The Royal Terrace offers traditional American dishes, and the Pilot House Sandwich Emporium, on the third floor of the casino, offers New Orleans-syle "po'boys," soups, salads, and snacks.

Club:	VIP Slot Club
Admission:	No admission charge
Hours:	24 hours a day, 7 days a week
Location:	Broadwater Beach Resort
	2110 Beach Blvd.
	Biloxi, MS 39531
Phone:	1-800-THE-PRES

LAKESHORE

Bayou Caddy's Jubilee Casino

Bayou Caddy's Jubilee Casino is a four-story New Orleans–style floating casino which is 240 feet long, 72 feet wide, and 76 feet high. The large casino features more than 40,000 square feet of gaming, including 60 game tables with craps, blackjack, and baccarat. In addition, there are 875 slot and video poker machines. The Poker Room offers Texas Hold 'Em, Seven-Card Stud, Carribean Stud, and Pai Gow poker. The casino is also well known in the area for its fresh and delicious Gulf seafood and great entertainment. A 400-seat showroom features top attractions every night, from New Orleans jazz masters to top country, blues, and rock legends. Everything has been elaborately designed and created to bring the patron a fun and memorable experience in the New Orleans tradition.

The casino is owned by Alpha Gulf Coast, Inc., a subsidiary of Alpha Hospitality Corporation. Other Alpha projects include the Fulton's Landing Resort at Rising Sun, Indiana.

The Jubilee Casino opened at the end of 1993 and is located just five miles from the Louisiana-Mississippi border and about thirty-five miles from New Orleans.

Club:	Jubilee Joe's Krewe (membership free)
Admission:	No admission charge
Hours:	24 hours a day, 365 days a year
Location:	5005 South Beach Blvd.
	Clermont Harbor
	Lakeshore, MS 39558
Phone:	1-800-552-0707

6

The Louisiana Boats

In 1991 Missouri and Louisiana both passed legislation making them the fourth and fifth states in the nation to allow riverboat gambling. The Louisiana Riverboat Economic Development and Gaming Control Act authorized licensing a maximum of fifteen riverboats, with the following restrictions: Each riverboat must be a newly constructed paddlewheeler, fully operational, at least 120 feet long, and able to carry a minimum of 600 people. The boats must be substantially in keeping with the appearance or aesthetics of historical designs of nineteenth-century riverboats. A New Orleans casino bill was passed

Shreveport Rose, Shreveport, Louisiana

by the state legislature in 1992, and proposals were solicited from interested companies for a land-based casino.

Getting a license for a riverboat from the state of Louisiana is not a simple matter. A $30,000 total application fee is required, as well as an economic development and utilization plan for the site and its surrounding areas. A list of projected employees, with job classifications and salaries, and a statement of local support or opposition are required, as well as a projected participation by any minority-owned or disadvantaged business enterprises. Detailed architectural plans for the boat, including a detailed artist's rendering, as well as a description of proposed support facilities, including an advertising plan, and detailed excursion plans are also necessary. After an application has been made and accepted, a preliminary certificate is issued by the gaming commission. It is not, however, a done deal until the casino has been licensed by the state police and a final certificate has been issued by the gaming commission. The decision by the state to limit the number of casino licenses will no doubt prove to have been a wise one.

You must be 21 to board any riverboat casino in Louisiana. The tax rate has been set at 18.5 percent.

BOSSIER CITY

Isle of Capri

The Isle of Capri in Bossier City opened in April 1994. Call 1-800-946-4753 for information.

Horseshoe Casino

The four-deck, 2,200-passenger Horseshoe riverboat is being built by Bender Shipyard at the time of this writing and is expected to open on Labor Day, 1994. Following Louisiana's laws, the 300-by-78-foot boat is a traditional Victorian-style paddlewheeler. With a total size of 93,000 square feet, the casino offers 30,000 square feet of actual gaming space, including 1,050 slot machines and 42 gaming tables.

The Horseshoe Pavilion is a two-story, 65,000-square-foot structure which houses two gift shops, a day care center, and a 250-seat lounge and features three restaurants with a total capacity of 650 seats. It joins the boat via enclosed climate-controlled boarding ramps, including a handicapped ramp. The overall cost for this fifteen-acre project is reported to be in excess of $65 million. Outside lighting alone is costing $1.25 million. The Horseshoe has a 126-foot revolving Horseshoe sign which reaches six stories above the top of the I-20 bridge. You can't miss it.

Club:	Call for information
Admission:	$2.50-per-person boarding fee
Hours:	24 hours a day, 365 days a year
Location:	415 Traffic St. at I-20
	Bossier City, LA 71111
Phone:	1-800-895-0711

SHREVEPORT

Harrah's Casino Shreveport

At the time of this writing, there is not much information available on this new Harrah's project. The casino's riverboat is named the Shreveport Rose. It is a traditional three-deck Victorian riverboat and is scheduled to cruise on Louisiana's Red River. This boat is scheduled to open April 15, 1994. As yet, no toll-free number has been assigned.

BATON ROUGE

Baton Rouge is a magnificent and historical Mississippi River city which is visited by more than 3.5 million people annually. It is the home of Louisiana State University, the USS *Kidd*, many regional fairs and festivals, dozens of plantation homes, some of the finest Cajun food in the world, and, now, the Casino Rouge Riverboat.

Baton Rouge, which in French means "red stick," was so named for the red stick stuck in the ground which served as a boundary between two Native American tribes. At least, that's the way legend has it. Actually, the area was settled mainly by French Acadians from Nova Scotia. Despite the overwhelming French influence, downtown Baton Rouge is divided into two sections. Spanish Town was settled originally by people from the Canary Islands who moved there after the Louisiana Purchase from their original colony southeast of Baton Rouge. Beauregard Town was a planned city development laid out in the European manner during the first decade of the nineteenth century. The area features a variety of distinct and unusual architectural influences.

Baton Rouge is also the capital of Louisiana. The state capitol, the tallest in the nation, is a thirty-four-story art deco building which houses a visitor information center as well as an observation deck. The visitor center should be the visitor's first stop. There one can get information on the dozens of interesting attractions and sights in the area, such as the casinos, the River Road plantations, the Old Governor's Mansion, and the Greater Baton Rouge Zoo.

For further information contact:

Baton Rouge Area Convention and Visitors' Bureau
P.O. Box 4149
Baton Rouge, LA 70821
Phone: 504-383-1825

Casino Rouge

Louisiana Casino Cruises' Casino Rouge, in Baton Rouge, is part of a $60 million, eighteen-acre development along the riverfront, which includes a paved, lighted walkway along the levee, an amphitheater, and other attractions. The 258-foot boat is a 60,000-square-foot turn-of-the-century paddlewheeler, with three enclosed decks and a covered hurricane deck on top. The Casino Rouge was built by the famed Bender Shipyards and has a cruising capacity of 1,500 passengers. It was delivered to the Baton Rouge site in June 1994, and cruise and gaming operations commenced shortly thereafter.

Casino space on Casino Rouge extends throughout all three decks and totals 28,000 square feet of actual gaming space. The lavishly appointed casino interior includes 850 slots and 45 game tables. The boat also houses restaurants, lounges, live entertainment, and a gift shop.

Louisiana Casino Cruises entered into an arrangement with Carnival Management Services, a subsidiary of Carnival Cruise Lines, whereby Carnival was responsible for training and hiring the more than 800 employees. The management contract also provided that Carnival would manage the overall operations of the Casino Rouge Riverboat as well as the dockside facilities. As part of this agreement, Casino Rouge becomes part of Carnival Cruise Lines' extensive nationwide travel network.

Club:	Club Rouge
Admission:	Not determined at time of writing
Hours:	Casino Rouge cruises 7 days a week with six 3-hour cruises each day. Call for specific information on boarding and departure times.
Location:	River Road (across from State Capitol Building) Baton Rouge, LA 70821
Phone:	504-922-9210. A toll-free number is expected soon.

Catfish Queen

The Catfish Queen is the second casino boat to open in Baton Rouge. This 266-foot riverboat offers an actual casino floor space of 29,082 square feet and provides 1,137 gaming positions, including a wide variety of electronic slots and videos as well as an excellent selection of table games. Scheduled to open in spring 1994.

Location:	France St. (Catfish Town) Baton Rouge, LA 70821
Phone:	504-344-8943. A toll-free number will be assigned in the future. Call directory assistance for number.

LAKE CHARLES

Players Riverboat Casino

Before we examine the Players Riverboat Casino in Lake Charles, we should talk about Merv Griffin, since he is a majority stock owner and spokesman for the Players Riverboat Casinos in both Lake Charles, Louisiana, and Metropolis, Illinois. Merv began his career singing with the Freddy Martin Orchestra, before becoming an actor for Warner Brothers. He ultimately found his true home on television, where he served twenty-three years as the host of the ever popular *Merv Griffin Show*, one of television's most successful and enduring programs. In addition to years of nightclub, stage, film, and television appearances, the ten-time Emmy winner created *Wheel of Fortune* and *Jeopardy*, the two most successful game shows in television history. Throughout his incredible career, Merv constantly bought and sold real estate, including radio stations and other properties. Eventually he bought the Beverly Hilton Hotel and now owns the Resorts Hotel/Casino in Atlantic City as well as the one at Paradise Island.

"The most exciting riverboat in Cajun country," Players Riverboat Casino is located on a ten-acre site on I-10 in Lake Charles. The riverboat site includes a hotel, two restaurants, a snack bar, and a gift shop. There is ample parking for buses and cars. The 3.4 million-pound ship was built by Leevac Shipyards in Jennings, Louisiana, over an eight-month period at a cost of $8.5 million.

The superstructure supports five decks, the first three of which are casino space. The fourth deck contains a snack bar as well as an observation area offering a panoramic view of Lake Charles and the Calcasieu River.

Owned by Players International, Inc. (NASDAQ: PLAY), this traditional 1,700-passenger boat, with a crew of 10 and over 200 employees, joins Players Riverboat in Metropolis, Illinois, as the company's second riverboat property. The 240-by-61-foot paddlewheeler, which opened in December 1993, offers 28,000 square feet of casino space, featuring over 800 slots and 45 gaming tables, including roulette wheels, craps tables, and Big Six. This casino is scaled for the middle- to upper-income consumer.

Restaurant facilities include the Celebrity Restaurant Buffet, which offers a delightful buffet, in addition to a full-service menu. The Celebrity Restaurant is particularly interesting in that the walls are covered with Hollywood photographs from Merv's personal collection. There is also Merv's Bar & Grill, which features a 27-foot solid mahogany bar, and serves Texas-style steaks and chops as well as meals with a Cajun flair. The excellent Players Gift Shop provides a varied selection of items with a riverboat theme.

The Players Lake Charles property is a classic example of the economic impact a casino opening can have on a given area. Players will add more than 900 jobs with a total annual payroll of $18 million to the local economy. Players is expected to host over 1.5 million visitors annually. Additionally, the casino's presence will mean increased revenues from associated developments in areas such as lodging, auto rentals, property improvements, taxes, etc.

Club: Players Club

Admission: $5.99–$10.00, with higher prices on weekends. Group inquiries are welcome, and group plans feature special greeters, incentive discount packages, special event opportunities, and convenient parking for more than 30 buses and 100 cars.

Hours: Continuous gaming 9:00 A.M. to 3:00 A.M. Cruises departing every 3 hours from 9:00 A.M. to midnight. The boat closes from 3:00 A.M. to 9:00 A.M. each day.

Location: 507 North Lakeshore Drive Lake Charles, LA 70601

Phone: 1-800-ASK-MERV for casino information 1-800-625-BOAT for group reservations 1-800-871-7666 for room accommodations

NEW ORLEANS

New Orleans, known as the Crescent City, is one of the world's great cities—birthplace of Dixieland and jazz, home of America's best food and best music—a place where anything and everything thrives. From the historic French Quarter and Mardi Gras, to the elegance of the Garden District, to the great plantation houses on River Road, this city has no equal. But New Orleans is more than a city, it is a state of being. Those who live there bathe in the aura of cultural diversity. Visitors return whenever possible for a good dose of culture. It is supremely appropriate that this magnificent city should serve as a base for several great riverboats. To those of you visiting for the first time, plan to stay awhile. You will want to visit Riverwalk, the Aquarium of the Americas, the Confederate Museum, the Gallier House, the Gumbo Shop, the French Market, Jax Brewery, Cafe du Monde, Magazine Street, and the Dixie Brewery.

Belle of New Orleans

Application for riverboat operation was made on behalf of Bally Louisiana, Inc., on April 12, 1993. The application was approved and a preliminary certificate was issued on January 28, 1994. No opening date has been set.

Crescent City Queen

Application to operate another New Orleans riverboat was made by Crescent City Capital Development in April 1993. The application was approved and a preliminary certificate was issued in January 1994. No opening date has been set.

Grand Palais

The Grand Palais is another Bender Shipyard project. The 360-by-99-by-14-foot boat is scheduled to be delivered to its home port of New Orleans in November 1994.

Queen of New Orleans

The 2,400-passenger Queen of New Orleans, at the Hilton, is owned by New Orleans Paddlewheels, Inc., and the Hilton New Orleans Corporation and is operated by the Hilton Nevada Corporation, Hilton Hotels Corporation, and the Hilton New Orleans Corporation. The interim riverboat took its maiden voyage on

February 10, 1994, but was replaced by a larger 322-foot boat in September 1994. The traditional turn-of-the-century boat was built by Equitable-Halter of New Orleans and has four decks, 800 slot machines, 32 table games, and 30,000 square feet of actual gaming space. Passengers are on board the boat for three hours, during which the boat cruises approximately an hour and a half.

Club:	Chips Players Club	
Admission:	$12 Sunday P.M.–Friday A.M.	
	$18 Friday P.M.–Sunday A.M.	

Hours:	*Boarding Times*	*Cruise Times*
	8:00 A.M.–8:45 A.M.	8:45 A.M.–10:15 A.M.
	10:15 A.M.–11:45 A.M.	11:45 A.M.–1:15 P.M.
	1:15 P.M.–2:45 P.M.	2:45 P.M.–4:15 P.M.
	4:15 P.M.–5:45 P.M.	5:45 P.M.–7:15 P.M.
	7:15 P.M.–8:45 P.M.	8:45 P.M.–10:15 P.M.
	10:15 P.M.–11:45 P.M.	11:45 P.M.–1:15 A.M.
	*1:15 A.M.–2:45 A.M.	*2:45 A.M.–4:15 A.M.

*Friday and Saturday (after midnight)

Schedules with this boat, as with all others, are subject to change without notice.

Note: Gaming begins 45 minutes before and continues 45 minutes after each cruise.

Location:	Poydras Street Wharf (behind the
	Hilton Hotel)
	New Orleans, LA 70130
Phone:	1-800-587-LUCK
	In New Orleans call 504-587-7777

Star Casino

The 265-by-78-foot Star Casino was built by famed Bender Ship-building in Briathwaite, Louisiana, and was delivered on October 23, 1993, making it Louisiana's first operational gaming vessel. The beautiful sternwheeler, with 22,000 square feet of actual gaming space, was completed in just seven and a half months, a record time. The riverboat, named for Preakness and Belmont winner Risen Star, is staffed with approximately 300 support staff members, in addition to a fulltime crew of 12.

The craft is powered by a 2200-horsepower engine which drives the sternwheel, producing a top speed of 11 knots. The traditional riverboat offers six cruises per day with each cruise providing nearly three and a half hours of actual gaming time. The cruise generally lasts two hours, with state law permitting another forty-five minutes of dockside gambling prior to and after each cruise.

The ship accommodates 1,250 passengers per run with an equal number of gaming positions, 760 of which are slot machines and the remainder of which are gaming tables. The interior of the star is as elaborate as anything Las Vegas has to offer. Gaming space is divided into two sections. In the general area, the extravagant interior features a gold ceiling with gold stanchions. Elevators transport passengers between the three decks, where there are extensive bars with inlaid poker machines. On the top, or Texas, deck, there is a VIP section, adjacent to which is an outside area covered with a canopy where passengers may relax and enjoy the view of the passing scenery. Dockside, there is a 34,000-square-foot shoreline pavilion which offers full entertainment, and food and beverage services for passengers waiting to board the vessel. The terminal building also houses an information and reservations booth, cage and credit office, a gift shop, and the security operations center. Corporate offices of the Star Casino are located on the second floor of the terminal building.

The security system at the Star Casino is absolute state-of-the-art, and the casino complex is monitored and patrolled twenty-four hours a day. Color video cameras survey every square inch of the parking area, the terminal, and the casino. An armed, uniformed security force combines both walking and vehicular patrols to ensure the safety of employees and guests.

The grand opening of the Star Casino was held on October 24, 1993, an invitation-only black-tie affair, which attracted 3,500 guests, VIPs, members of the Louisiana Gaming Commission, and local officials. The guests were treated to catered food, gaming entertainment, and live music from The Four Tops.

Club: Star Club

Admission: No admission charge

Hours:	The Star Casino is open 24 hours a day, 7 days a week. It does not have a dockside season but sometimes stays dockside anyway, for one reason or another. When the boat is dockside, passengers may come aboard and leave whenever they please. The average cruise lasts approximately 90 minutes. If patrons wish to stay on board, they may remain as long as they wish.
Cruise schedule:	10 A.M., 1:00 P.M., 4:00 P.M., 7:00 P.M., 10:00 P.M., 1:00 A.M.
Location:	1 Star Casino Blvd. (At Star Casino Terminal, South Shore Harbor on Lake Pontchartrain) New Orleans, LA 70126
Phone:	1-800-504-STAR

KENNER (A NEW ORLEANS SUBURB)

Treasure Chest

The Treasure Chest is another Bender Shipyard project. The 260-by-78-by-14-foot boat is scheduled to be delivered in May 1994, will operate out of North Kenner, a New Orleans suburb, and will cruise Lake Pontchartrain. The 1,800-passenger boat has three decks.

Phone:	1-800-750-5777

CHALMETTE

American Entertainment

American Entertainment has applied for a license and was granted a preliminary certificate on January 28, 1994. The boat is a partnership between Circus Circus and American Entertainment

Corporation and is scheduled to cruise on Bayou Bienvenue. At the time of this writing, no other information is available, and the boat has not yet been named.

HARVEY

Boomtown Belle

The Boomtown Belle is a western-themed riverboat casino located at Boomtown Westbank, in Harvey, Louisiana. The Old West theme extends throughout every phase of the operation, from the land-based pavilion to the boat, inside and out. The Boomtown Belle was constructed by Avondale Shipyard in Westwego, Louisiana, at a cost of more than $14 million. The 250-by-72-foot boat has a total passenger and crew capacity of 1,600. The riverboat casino has an actual overall gaming area of 28,000 square feet, which includes 872 slot machines and 51 table games, including 40 blackjack, 7 craps, and 4 roulette tables.

The $17 million dockside facility was built by Grimaldi Construction Company and contains a restaurant, lounge, cabaret, and a Family Fun Center.

Club:	Call for information
Admission:	No admission charge at time of writing
Hours:	Call for information
Location:	2439 Manhattan Harvey, LA 70059
Phone:	1-800-366-7711

ST. CHARLES PARISH

Casino St. Charles

Casino St. Charles is owned by St. Charles Gaming Company, a subsidiary of Crown Casino Corporation, and will be located in St. Charles Parrish, about ten miles west of New Orleans. The 270-by-70-foot boat is being built by Kehl at the time of this writing and is scheduled to open in May 1994. The casino will contain 775 slot machines and 40 table games. No toll-free number has been assigned yet.

Louisiana Gaming Division

Louisiana Gaming Division
625 North 4th St.
Baton Rouge, LA 70804
Phone: 504-342-2465

7

The Missouri Boats

On April 30, 1993, C. J. Lawrence's *Gaming Weekly* predicted that Missouri's statewide gaming revenues would eventually reach $1 billion, making Missouri the largest gaming market outside of Las Vegas and Atlantic City. The Missouri Senate amended original legislation in order to leave it up to individual cities whether boats would have to cruise or would be permitted to remain dockside. The original $500-per-person loss limit was also removed, and regulations limiting the amount of space which a casino could devote to gambling were removed as well.

Casino Queen, East St. Louis, Illinois

In a late-breaking bombshell, the Missouri Supreme Court decided that some popular games were illegal according to its interpretation of the laws. Amidst a great deal of judicial chatter and legal mumbo jumbo, it was decided, at least for the moment, that games such as poker and blackjack, considered to be games of skill, are legal, while other games of pure chance, such as craps and slot machines, are not. What this means, after all the smoke has settled, is that as of this writing, there are several riverboat casinos in operation but none with slot machines yet.

There are, however, according to the Missouri Gaming Commission, twenty-two applications on file. The Gaming Commission is supposed to meet sometime this year to review applications and consider licenses.

Among some of those applicants are the following:

KIMMSWICK

Lady Luck Gaming corporation purchased the Cajun Magic, a 320-by-96-foot vessel, for its operations in Missouri. The boat will be docked twenty miles south of St. Louis and includes a hotel and entertainment center on the forty-five-acre dockside site. The projected cost is $55 million.

ST. LOUIS

Harrah's St. Louis/Maryland Heights

On June 18, 1993, Harrah's announced plans for a riverboat casino on a seventy-one-acre site in the St. Louis suburb of Maryland Heights. Harrah's signed a letter of intent with Sverdup Investments to enter into a joint venture to create a ninety-two-acre multifaceted entertainment destination adjacent to the riverboat site. The traditional paddlewheeler will have an overall size of 43,000 square feet, with a total casino area of 32,000 square feet housing 1,460 slot machines and 54 table games. Harrah's investment in the site and riverboat totals $82 million. Scheduled to open in late 1994.

The President on the Admiral

Dockside gaming was authorized for the city of St. Louis in November 1992, and the President Casino expects to open aboard the riverboat *Admiral* in 1994. The boat now known as the *Admiral* was originally christened the SS *Albatross* in 1907 and served as a ferry from 1907 to 1937. Between the years of 1937 and 1940, the boat was reconstructed, and it emerged in June 1940 as a dining and entertainment cruise ship. The *Admiral* served St. Louis residents for over forty years as a dining and entertainment cruise ship. the mammoth 400-by-90-foot *Admiral* was renovated at a cost of more than $28 million, and can hold up to 4,000 guests. The boat has a total of five decks, three of which will be used as casino space, with a total gaming area in excess of 70,000 square feet. The casino features a giant atrium with 1,500 slot machines, and 60 table games, including blackjack, craps, roulette, Wheel of Fortune, and more.

Restaurant services include the Crystal Terrace Restaurant, specializing in steaks, chops, and seafood, as well as lighter, more casual fare. The Food Court is noted for a wide selection of fast-food items, and the Upper Deck serves a wide selection of favorite regional dishes.

The *Admiral* is located right under the world-famous Gateway Arch, and within walking distance of Busch Stadium, the new Cervantes Convention Center, and downtown hotels, restaurants, and offices.

Note: The President is a dockside casino only, and does not cruise.

Club:	As yet unnamed
Admission:	As yet undetermined
Hours:	7:00 A.M.–3:00 A.M. The boat boards at specific times for gaming sessions. Call for information.
Location:	802 North 1st St. St. Louis, MO 63102
Phone:	1-800-787-7711 or 314-622-3000

KANSAS CITY

Harrah's North Kansas City Riverboat Casino

This riverboat casino is located three miles from downtown Kansas City, Missouri, and is expected to open in 1994. The gaming area exceeds 30,000 square feet of actual casino space and includes 1,100 slot and video poker machines and 55 gaming tables. The 60,000-square-foot dockside facility features a speciality-theme restaurant, lounge, amusement center, and ticketing and staging areas.

Missouri Gaming Commission

Considering the strange state of affairs as far as riverboat gaming is concerned in Missouri, it is suggested that the gaming visitor contact the Missouri Gaming Commission at the number below prior to making any specific travel plans.

Missouri Gaming Commission
11775 Borman Drive #104
St. Louis, MO 63146
Phone: 314-340-4400

8

The Illinois Boats

Illinois, along with Mississippi, legalized riverboat gambling in 1990 and, like Mississippi, is prime territory for the new riverboats. In addition to the large population base, Illinois has no state-imposed betting limits or gaming restrictions, and has set at ten the number of licenses (two boats per license) which it will issue to casinos. Under current law, slots must pay out between 80 percent and 100 percent. The downside is the state's 20 per-

Silver Eagle, E. Dubuque, Illinois

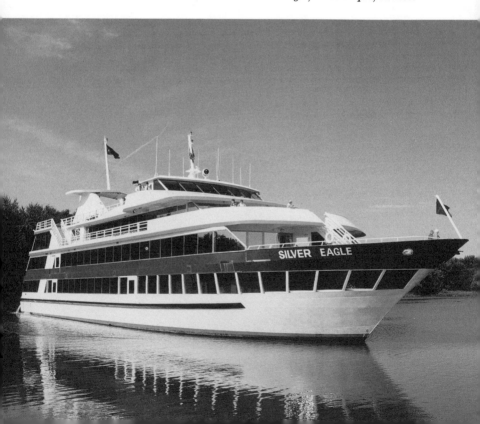

cent tax rate. All told, the presence of the riverboats in Illinois has been directly responsible for the creation of more than 10,000 new jobs already, with an estimated yearly payroll for all of the boats in excess of $250 million. Each boat adds an average $39,000 a day in new state taxes and $16,000 in new local taxes—that's a $55,000 per boat per day. These figures do not include the millions of dollars spent by the more than 12.5 million annual visitors to the Illinois riverboats, who not only play the casinos but spend other money on hotels, restaurants, shops, and other attractions.

It is important to note that while visitors are permitted to enjoy dining, shopping, or browsing at dockside facilities, state laws require that anyone boarding the riverboats be at least 21 years of age.

ALTON

Alton Belle II

The Alton Belle II is owned by Argosy Gaming, an Illinois company, and was the first riverboat to open in Illinois waters. The original Alton Belle, a smaller boat, opened for business on September 10, 1991, but was replaced by the Alton Belle II in May 1993. The new 220-by-66-foot boat was constructed by Atlantic Marine in Jacksonville, Florida, and has a cruising capacity of 1,300 passengers. The casino houses 650 slot, video poker, and electronic keno machines and has 32 table games, including blackjack, 1 Big Six wheel, 4 craps tables, and 3 roulette wheels. Food and beverage services on board include two seated bars as well as a deli.

The Alton Belle II weighs over 3,430,000 pounds, is covered with 4,100 gallons of paint, has 180,000 lightbulbs, 310,000 feet of electrical cable, and requires a 260-ton air-conditioning system.

In many cases, the dockside facilities equal the riverboats in grandeur. Dockside facilities at the Alton Belle II are no exception, and consist of a three-story structure called Alton Landing. The first floor houses a gift shop, ticket sales, information, a bar, and the VIP Argosy Room for Alton Belle Platinum Card holders. The second floor serves mainly as a dining facility, with Ace's Sport Lounge and a food court. Belle's Buffet, a lounge, and Victor's, a fine-food restaurant, are located on the third level.

Note: There is no specific dockside season as such, but the boat may remain dockside at the discretion of the captain if weather is threatening. In such cases, gaming continues dockside. All cruise schedules and admission prices are subject to change without notice.

Club:	Best Bet Club. This slot club offers free membership. Best Bet Club members who earn 100,000 points are presented a platinum card which entitles the bearer to admission into the Argosy Room, a private room located on the first floor of the Alton Landing dockside facility.
Admission:	All cruises are $4 at the time of this writing.
Hours:	Cruises daily every two hours beginning at 9:00 A.M. and continuing through 11:00 P.M. On Friday and Saturday there is an extra 1:00 A.M. cruise.
Location:	1 Piasa St. Alton, IL 62002
Phone:	1-800-336-7568, reservations and general information; 1-800-253-3423, group sales

AURORA

Hollywood Casino

Aurora, Illinois, located thirty-eight miles west of Chicago along Route 88, is the home of the Hollywood Casino complex, perhaps the most unique of all the riverboat casinos. The Hollywood Casino is "a blend of the complete Las Vegas experience and the grandeur of Hollywood's golden era." There are actually two riverboat casinos located at this facility, City of Lights I and City of Lights II. These boats were named in honor of Aurora, known as the City of Lights, the first city in the world to light the streets entirely with electricity. Each of the 600-passenger, 145-foot-by-45-foot riverboat casinos has four decks, 20,000 square feet of enclosed space, and 10,600 square feet of actual casino space. Both boats have a casino on each deck, with 300 slot and video games. Table games on each boat include 4 roulette wheels, 21 blackjack tables, 4 craps tables, 1 baccarat table, and 1 mini-baccarat table.

The twin boats were designed by the firm of Dejong and Lebet, of Jacksonville, Florida, and were constructed by Maritime Systems Designs, of Morgan City, Louisiana, and Garbe Iron Works, of Aurora. The casinos opened in June 1993 and travel the Fox River, between the New York Street Bridge and the Illinois Avenue Bridge.

Dockside facilities consist of the Hollywood Casino's ornate art deco Pavilion, which serves as the entry to the two casinos. This unique and interesting four-story, 65,000-square-foot building follows the same architectural theme as the nearby Paramount Arts Theatre and houses a variety of restaurants, bars, a gift shop, and ticketing and holding facilities.

Fairbanks and Rudolfo's. Located side by side on the fourth level of the Pavilion are Rudolfo's and Fairbanks restaurants. Rudolfo's Ristorante Italiano, inspired by Rudolph Valentino, brings a true taste of Northern Italian cuisine to Aurora. The 140-seat restaurant is beautifully decorated with paintings of Italian villas and serves a wide selection of exquisite Italian dishes.

Hours are 5:00 P.M. to 10:30 P.M. Monday, Tuesday, and Sunday; 5:00 P.M. to 10:30 P.M. Friday and Saturday; the restaurant is closed Wednesday and Thursday. Reservations are recommended and may be obtained by calling the casino's main number: 1-800-888-7777.

Fairbanks, "a Swashbuckling Steakhouse," has a capacity of 100 persons and is modeled after the great Chicago-style steakhouses. The menu features a wide variety of aged prime cuts of steak, prime rib of beef, and a 48-ounce porterhouse for the diner with a truly large appetite. Additionally, Fairbanks offers an excellent selection of fresh seafood. Hours are 5:00 P.M. to 10:30 P.M. Tuesday through Saturday; the restaurant is closed Sunday and Monday. Reservations are recommended and may be obtained by calling the casino's main number: 1-800-888-7777.

Cafe Harlow. Cafe Harlow is the Hollywood Casino's gourmet restaurant and features a wide selection of classic dishes, perfectly prepared and exquisitely presented in an excellent and intimate atmosphere. Surrounding the restaurant is Club Harlow, an upscale lounge which offers great mixed drinks and cocktails, as well as a great view of the Fox River. Hours are 5:30 P.M. to 10:30 P.M. Tuesday, Wednesday, and Thursday; 5:00 P.M. to 10:30 P.M. Friday and Saturday; the restaurant is closed Sunday and Monday. Reservations are required and can be obtained by calling the casino's main number: 1-800-888-7777.

Hollywood Epic Buffet. Located on the first level of the Pavilion, the Hollywood Epic Buffet is a 250-seat buffet overlooking the Fox River. The menu includes an excellent selection of pasta, meats, seafoods, fruits, vegetables, salads, and desserts. The Epic serves breakfast, lunch, and dinner, and opens at 8:30 A.M. for breakfast and 11:00 A.M. for lunch Monday through Saturday; closing is at 11:00 P.M. Sunday through Thursday and midnight on Friday and Saturday; Sunday hours are 10:00 A.M. to 11:00 P.M.

Take One. Located on the first level of the Pavilion, Take One is the perfect choice for guests on the go. Featured selections include hot dogs, roast beef sandwiches, Chicago-style pizza, ice cream, and Italian ice. Hours are 10:00 A.M. to midnight Sunday through Thursday, and 10:00 A.M. til 2:00 A.M. Friday and Saturday.

Like everything else at the Hollywood Casino, the Pavilion has been designed to transport the visitor into another dimension, one outside the realm of the ordinary. With its winding stairways, breathtaking atrium, and incredible decor, the Pavilion succeeds admirably. Hollywood memorabilia is displayed throughout the Pavilion, and exhibits include unique and interesting personal items from famous Hollywood celebrities, such as John Wayne's cowboy hat, Jean Harlow's Oscar for lifetime achievement, Jimmy Stewart's jacket and bow tie from the movie *Harvey*, Charlton Heston's Roman toga from *Ben Hur*, and much more.

The Golden Era Shop, also located in the Pavilion, is an excellent gift shop which offers movie posters, videotapes, books, and other Hollywood and movie memorabilia for sale.

The Hollywood theme continues throughout every aspect of the casino complex, from the dazzling art deco interior appointments to the uniforms of the staff and employees, even to the roaming costumed impersonators who resemble some of the movie world's most famous actors.

The Paramount Arts Theatre, built in 1931, is less than 100 yards away from the Hollywood Casino and is connected to the casino property by a walkway. Visitors to the Hollywood Casino will want to check out the top names performing at this world-famous venue.

Club:	There is a slot club which offers free membership, cards, and other benefits. Call for information.
Admission:	Prices range from $2 for the 1:00 A.M. cruise to $15 for certain Friday and Saturday evening cruises. Most weekday cruises, however, are $5.
Hours:	Cruises are scheduled from 8:30 A.M. throughout the day and evening, with the last one departing at 1:00 A.M. *Note:* While there is no dockside season as such, the boat does not cruise in bad weather. Gaming continues while the boat is docked, but boarding follows the same schedule as with cruises. In other words, while the passenger may leave the boat at any time, boarding is only permitted at designated times.
Note:	Pricing and scheduling are subject to change without notice.
Location:	1 New York Street Bridge Aurora, IL
Phone:	1-800-888-7777. This phone number is regional and does not necessarily work from all areas. In the event that it does not work from your area, try 708-801-7000.

EAST DUBUQUE

Silver Eagle

The Silver Eagle opened June 17, 1992, and has been going
strong ever since. The sleek and modern 205-foot boat was originally a dinner cruise ship based in San Francisco, and was converted to a casino and moved to Illinois. It is open 9:00 A.M. to
1:00 A.M. and generally runs six cruises daily, with a shorter
cruise schedule in the winter months. The 1,000-passenger vessel
has 470 slots, 24 blackjack tables, 3 craps tables, and 2 roulette
wheels. The vessel offers unlimited-stakes gambling, cocktail service, and an incredible three-deck atrium.

The Eagle's Nest Pavilion is the Silver Eagle's home base and
contains gift and apparel shops, breakfast, lunch, and dinner service, beverage service, and two outdoor patios. the Silver Eagle
also offers group rates and a private room for meetings and
receptions.

Club:	Eagle Advantage Club; call for information.
Admission:	Admission is $3 on weekdays, but escalates to $5 on Friday evenings and between $5 and $7 on Saturdays. Group rates are available. Call for information.
Hours:	Boarding begins Sunday through Thursday at 10:30 A.M. Cruises start at 11:00 A.M. and run approximately every two hours, with the last cruise starting at 10:30 P.M. On Friday and Saturday, the last cruise begins at 12:30 A.M. *Note:* While there is no specific dockside season as such, the boat is generally dockside in cold weather and when the water is frozen and navigation is difficult.

EAST PEORIA

Par-A-Dice

The story of the 1,200-person, capacity Par-A-Dice Riverboat Casino in East Peoria, Illinois, is a perfect example of what a riverboat can mean to a city if everything is properly handled. On June 26, 1990, a group consisting of twenty-two mostly local investors formed the Greater Peoria Riverboat Corporation for the purpose of starting a riverboat casino. In May 1991 the group purchased the former Peoria Boatworks site, and by November 20, 1992, the riverboat was in operation. In the meantime, construction was underway at the docking facility. The City of Peoria invested $1.2 million to provide streets, lighting, landscaping, and sewer, water, and gas lines at the site. Within less than a year, the city had recouped all of its initial expenditures strictly from gaming revenues generated by the Par-A-Dice project, without any burden on the taxpayers.

The boat itself, originally named the Golden Lady, was designed by John Gilbert of Boston, built by Atlantic Marine in Jacksonville, Florida, and scheduled for service in Iowa, the first state to legalize riverboat gaming. It was, however, diverted and purchased by GPRC, renamed the Par-A-Dice, and placed in service at East Peoria, five months ahead of schedule. During this advance period, the boat drew 386,000 customers and generated $5.4 million in state and local taxes. All in all, the Par-A-Dice drew more than a million guests in the first eleven months. The projected gross revenue for the boat was $32 million during the first year of operation. The casino actually reached the $32 million figure after only seven months in business. After two years on the water, the Par-A-Dice is grossing over $70 million a year and attracts over a million and a half visitors a year.

The Greater Peoria Riverboat Corporation's total investment in the Par-A-Dice project to date is approximately $37 million, including the following:

$15 million for the purchase of the riverboat, gaming
    equipment, and furnishings
$6 million to purchase and renovate the former Peoria
    Boatworks, as a temporary docking site for Par-A-Dice

$1 million to purchase land at the East Peoria site
$5 million total investment to date in site
$4 million preopening expenses (prior to November 20, 1991)
$1 million to dredge river channel for the East Peoria dock
$5 million to complete construction of the East Peoria land base.

While the riverboat currently takes in an average monthly gaming win in excess of $5 million, it has accomplished much more than just increasing the city and state tax base. In addition to having nearly one thousand employees, the Par-A-Dice has involved local businesses from the outset in almost every phase of operations, from financing, design, construction, and furnishing, to the purchase of local services and labor. The Fondulac Bank of East Peoria provided the initial financing for the development of the East Peoria land base. Secondary financing was provided through a joint effort between the City of East Peoria and Community Banks of Greater Peoria. Schielein Construction, of Peoria, was secured as general contractor.

Modeled along the lines of the successful nineteenth-century Hudson and Queen City riverboats, the 228-by-46-foot Par-A-Dice is a traditional sternwheeler with three 670-horsepower Caterpillar diesel engines. In addition to the powered rear paddlewheel, the boat is powered by two propellers known in nautical terms as "screws." It has 71 doors, 206 windows, holds 15,200 gallons of fuel, 400 gallons of oil, 9,400 gallons of water, two 715-kilowatt generators, and has four decks. The main deck houses slot machines, general offices, restrooms, a lobby, a bar, an auxiliary generator room, and an open forward deck. The boiler deck, or second level, contains game tables, slot machines, a bar, restrooms, open side decks, and an open forward deck. The third level, or Texas Deck as it is usually called, contains a no-smoking casino, a bar, restrooms, a forward lounge, an open deck with passenger seating. On top of the Texas Deck is the pilothouse, which is the main control center of the vessel and contains the steering, propulsion, and navigation controls.

All told, the casino has a total of 804 gaming positions, including 567 slot and video machines, 32 blackjack, 4 craps, and 3 roulette tables, 1 Big Six wheel, and 1 mini-baccarat table. The Par-A-Dice Pavilion is a 42,800-square-foot building which provides a permanent docking site for the Par-A-Dice riverboat casino and also houses administrative offices, ticketing facilities, a gift shop, a boarding area, two restaurants, and a cocktail lounge. The Pavilion was designed by Darren Wright of Ultimate Interiors, and follows an art deco theme. The 380-seat Broadway Buffet, located in the pavilion, is open seven days a week, serving all-you-can-eat breakfast, lunch, and dinner. A wide selection of excellent buffet selections is available for each meal. Breakfast, at $4.95, is served from 7:30 A.M. to 10:00 A.M.; lunch, at $6.95, is served from 10:30 A.M. to 4:00 P.M.; and dinner, at $10.95, is served from 4:30 P.M. to 10:00 P.M.

The Boulevard Grille, also in the Pavilion, is an upscale steak house which is open seven days a week, serving lunch and dinner only. The house specialties include the finest prime meats and fresh fish. Reservations are recommended. Lunch is served from 1:00 A.M. to 3:00 P.M.; dinner is served from 4:30 P.M. to 10:00 P.M.

Flappers is an informal gathering spot located in the lobby of the Par-A-Dice Pavilion. For cocktails, sports scores, snacks, and a nice view of the river, this is the place to be.

The New Boat. Due to the outrageous success of the boat described above, a new, even larger Par-A-Dice began service in the spring of 1994. The $11 million vessel, like its predecessor, was built by Atlantic Marine in Jacksonville, Florida. The naval architect in this case was the company of Rodney Lay and Associates, also from Jacksonville. The new 260-by-66-foot ultramodern boat has a flat hull with a simulated catamaran bow for sleeker lines. The new craft has a 1,600-person capacity and offers 33,000 square feet of actual casino space, more than twice the size of casino space on the first boat. The state allows a maximum of 1,200 gaming positions, a figure which the new boat reaches with ease. Customer service on the new boat was also expanded to include cage facilities (for making change), bars and

lounge areas on each deck, and bar-mounted slot machines. The
new boat, like the first, is totally handicapped accessible.

The Greater Peoria Riverboat Corporation changed its name
to Par-A-Dice Gaming Corporation in late 1993 for better recognition within the gaming industry and as a preface to the possibility of expansion into other states.

Club: Club Par-A-Dice. Members of Club Par-
         A-Dice earn points every time they use
         their club card to play slots. Club Par-
         A-Dice members may redeem points for
         any dollar value over $1.00.
         Redemption certificates are just like
         cash and may be used anywhere in the
         casino.

Hours: *Boarding Begins*   *Cruise*
          8:30 A.M.   9–11:00 A.M.
          11:30 A.M.   Noon–2:00 P.M.
          2:30 P.M.   3–5:00 P.M.
          5:30 P.M.   6–8:00 P.M.
          8:30 P.M.   9–11:00 P.M.
          11:30 P.M.   Midnight–2:00 A.M.

Note: While there is no specific dockside season, the
boat remains dockside and does not cruise in bad or
threatening weather.

Admission: Sunday–Friday $4

              Saturday 9:00 A.M. $4

              Saturday (Except 9:00 A.M.) $9

              Seniors $2 discount on all cruises

Taxes included in admission price. Boarding tickets
may be purchased through Ticketmaster in Illinois, or
at the casino.

Location: 21 Blackjack Blvd.
             East Peoria, IL 61611

Phone: 1-800-Par*A*Dice; group reservations:
          1-800-4 FUN 777

EAST ST. LOUIS

Casino Queen

The Casino Queen is a massive 70,000-square-foot casino located in East St. Louis, Illinois, directly across the Mississippi River from the famous St. Louis Arch, in Missouri. This mammoth 2,500-passenger riverboat casino is the world's longest, with a total length of 447 feet, and an impressive beam (width) of 70 feet. It was built by the Patti Shipyard, and is actually a 330-foot passenger barge hooked to a 117-foot power plant. It was converted in 1991 from another ship known as the Admiral and now has over 1,200 gaming positions, including 850 slots.

The Casino Queen docks beside the 42,000-square-foot visitor's center, modeled after the old brick warehouses which were prevalent along the waterfront in the nineteenth century.

Club:	Slot Club	
Admission:	See below	
Hours:	9:30 A.M.	$3
	12:30 P.M.	$5
	3:30 P.M.	$5
	6:30 P.M.	$5
	9:30 P.M.	$5
	12:30 A.M.	$5
	3:30 A.M.	$2

Boarding begins 30 minutes prior to departure. All passengers must be on board by 25 minutes past the hour. All cruises are 3 hours, except for the 3:30 A.M. cruise, which is 2 hours in duration.

Note: While there is no specific dockside season, the boat is docked during bad weather.

Location:	200 South Front Street
	East St. Louis, IL 62201
Phone:	1-800-777-0777; group sales,
	1-800-933-ARCH

ELGIN

Elgin Riverboat Resort

The Elgin Riverboat Resort is an extensive undertaking resulting from a partnership agreement between Hyatt and the Nevada Landing Corporation. The traditional 400-by-100-foot sidewheeler was built by Bender Shipyards and opened in October 1994. The 1,200-passenger boat has two decks, both with casinos, boasting a total of 1,088 slot and video games and 30 table games, contained within an overall casino area in excess of 30,000 square feet.

The dockside facilities are housed in a two-story, 83,000-square-foot Victorian-themed building which contains a gourmet restaurant, a food court, sports bar, beverage services, a gift shop, and ticketing services.

Club:	Slot club as yet unnamed
Admission:	As yet undetermined
Hours:	Open for 6 cruises daily. Call for schedule. *Note:* The boat, like all Illinois boats, is scheduled to cruise all year, but may remain dockside during bad weather.
Location:	250 South Grove Elgin, IL 60120
Phone:	708-622-2704. There will be a toll-free number, but it is not available at the time of this writing.

JOLIET

Empress Casinos

The Empress I and Empress II are sleek, ultramodern vessels, located in Joliet, less than fifty miles from Chicago. As part of the new breed of streamlined and futuristic boats, the Empress boats are equipped with state-of-the-art everything. The Empress I completed its maiden voyage in June 1992. It is a double-deck boat, with an actual casino space of 16,837 square feet. In terms of the boats' gaming potential, there are over 600 slot and video games, 4 roulette wheels, 2 baccarat tables, 35 blackjack tables, and 5 craps tables. The boat is 222 by 67 feet, and has a passenger capacity of 1,200. In December 1993 the Empress I was joined by her sister ship, the Empress II. The Empress II is a triple-deck boat with an actual casino space of 19,429 square feet. The Empress II is slightly larger than her sister ship, with a passenger capacity of 1,500. Both boats offer an observation area on top of the boat, and together offer fourteen daily gaming sessions, seven days a week.

The original rural, wooded dockside pavilion was replaced in mid-1994 by an incredible new $40 million facility appropriately named the Empress Palace. This magnificent structure follows an ancient Egyptian theme, from giant seated pharaohs to twin obelisks and pyramids. Included in the new Empress Palace is Alexandria, fine dining at its best, as well as Rick's Cafe, the Marrakesh Market Food Court,and the Grand Ballroom. Everything about both of these boats and the dockside pavilion represents the best of the new riverboat casinos.

Club:	Empress Club
Admission:	Admission prices vary from $2 to $10
Hours:	Cruises operate daily from 7:30 A.M. to 3:00 A.M. *Note:* There is no specific dockside season, but the boats do not cruise in bad weather.
Location:	2300 Empress Drive Joliet, Illinois 60436
Phone:	708-345-6789. At the time of this writing there is no toll-free number. Group Sales: 815-744-1671.

Harrah's

Harrah's has two boats at the property in Joliet. The Northern Star, which opened in May 1993, is a brightly colored, incredibly futuristic 1,200-passenger boat. Built by Service Marine Industries in Morgan City, Louisiana, the three-level boat has a large atrium through the second and third floors, which is crowned by a huge crystal chandelier, with multilighting capabilities. A glass elevator adds to the ambiance. In addition to the unusual atrium, there are other interesting architectural features as well. Large, illuminated, multicolored beams extend floor to ceiling. Harrah's has gone to great expense to provide an almost completely smoke-free environment throughout the casino, with smoking not permitted on the second floor. The Northern Star has 570 slots and 43 game tables.

The Southern Star, Harrah's other Joliet boat, is a giant 1,200-passenger traditional sternwheeler. The massive boat, like its sister ship, was built by Service Marine and has three full decks, as well as an open top deck. It entered service in early 1994. Both boats are located downtown in an area which has recently undergone considerable renovation.

Club:	There is a Gold Card VIP club; call for information.
Admission:	Admission prices are $4, $10, and $15, depending on time and day of cruise.
Hours:	Northern Star cruises depart every 3 hours, beginning daily at 10:30 A.M., with the last cruise leaving at 1:30 A.M.
	Southern Star cruises depart every three hours, beginning daily at 9:00 A.M., with the last cruise at 12:00 midnight. There is a 3:00 A.M. cruise on weekends.

Note: There is no specific dockside season, but the boats remain in port in bad weather.

Location:	North 150 Joliet St. Joliet, IL 60431
Phone:	1-800-427-7247

METROPOLIS

PLAYER'S

Players International, Inc., is a public company (NASDAQ: PLAY) which entered the casino cruise ship business in 1989. Players

Riverboat Casino at Merv Griffin's Landing in Metropolis, Illinois, represents the company's first venture into riverboat gambling. The company opened a second Players Riverboat at a site in Lake Charles, Louisiana, in 1993 (see Chapter 10). Some of the services offered by Players International's related companies include:

Players Club International. This club provides a number of member privileges, including discounts on rooms, meals, and entertainment in a number of casinos and resorts worldwide.

Cash Advance Marketing. Cash Advance Marketing, an affiliated company, offers cash advances to gaming patrons against their major credit card accounts at casinos throughout America.

Players World Travel. This full-service international travel agency is designed exclusively for Players Club members and gaming enthusiasts.

International Gaming Promotions. Through its International Gaming Promotions affiliate, Players Club sponsors more than a dozen high-profile tournaments each year. These events include poker, blackjack, craps, slots, and other games of chance and sporting events, and take place in Las Vegas, Reno, and the Caribbean, as well as on cruise ships.

Players Riverboat Casino

Players Riverboat Casino is situated at Merv Griffin's Landing on the Ohio River in Metropolis, Illinois. The small riverside town of Metropolis (population a 6,732) is best known as the self-proclaimed home of DC comic hero Superman. While the community itself is small, there is within a 200-mile-radius a population base of approximately 8 million people, from southern Illinois, Kentucky, Tennessee, southern Indiana, and southern Missouri. The 1,400-passenger, 20,000-square-foot Players Riverboat Casino opened in the spring of 1993 and operates with an on-board crew of 42 and a large additional staff of casino employees. The $18.5 million, 210-by-60-foot riverboat was built by Leevac Shipyards in Jennings, Louisiana, and took ten months to complete. It is one of the largest boats of its type, with a total weight of 3.2 million pounds. It is interesting that despite the massive size of this vessel, it only displaces 5-1/2 feet of water. This low displacement is

characteristic of many of the riverboats and is the result of a very
shallow hull. Players offers Las Vegas–style gambling on the Ohio
River. The traditional riverboat has a Victorian interior and features 634 slot and video poker machines from 5 cents up. In addition,there are 28 blackjack tables, 2 roulette wheels, 1 Big Six
wheel.

Merv Griffin's Landing. Merv Griffin's Landing, the docking
facility and point of departure for Players Riverboat Casino, consists of former riverboat Belle Angeline, a permanently moored
structure, which houses Merv's Bar and Grill. This restaurant features a 40-foot mahogany bar flanked by a wall of windows
which looks out over the river. In this setting, exhibition-style
cooking of standard grill items takes on a new flavor.

The Celebrity Buffet, also housed within the 10,000-square-
foot kitchen and dining area, features a wide assortment of delicious items such as roast beef and prime rib. The atmosphere is
enhanced by a large selection of celebrity photographs taken
from Merv's years as a television talk show host.

Club:	Players Club	
Admission:	The admission price varies, and sometimes there are month-long specials. Seniors (55 and over) always receive a $2 discount off full regular fare.	
Hours:	*Sunday through Friday:*	
	9:00 A.M.	$2
	12:00 Noon, 3:00 P.M., & 6:00 p.m.	$10
	9:00 P.M.	$4
	Friday Midnight	$4
	Saturday	
	10:00 A.M.	$8
	12:00 Noon & 9:00 P.M.	$12
	Midnight	$4

Cruises depart every 3 hours from 9:00 A.M. to
midnight from Merv Griffin's Landing. The boat is
closed daily between the hours of 3:00 A.M. and

9:00 A.M. Due to the incredible popularity of this boat, reservations are accepted and suggested. Gaming activity is continuous, so patrons may buy "back-to-back" cruise packages. *Note:* There is no dockside season, but the boat does not cruise in bad weather.

Location: 207 South Ferry
Metropolis, IL 62960

Phone: 1-800-935-7700; group reservations
1-800-935-1111

ROCK ISLAND

Jumer's Casino Rock Island

The Casino Rock Island is another of the more traditional designs associated with the Mississippi steamboat era. The 200-by-54-foot sternwheeler opened in 1992 and has three enclosed decks, 400 slots, 18 blackjack tables, 4 craps tables, and 1 roulette wheel. Free soft drinks, hors d'oeuvres, and a $1 bar are available on each deck.

The Rock Island Casino has no on-shore facilities in the usual sense, but instead docks next to another boat known as the Effie Aston. This boat houses a restaurant and serves food daily between the hours of 11:00 A.M. and 7:30 P.M.

Club: Paddlewheel Club; Call for information

Admission: Prices range from $4 to $10, depending on time of day and day of the week.

Hours: 8:00 A.M., 10:00 A.M., 1:00 P.M., 3:00 P.M., 5:00 P.M., 7:00 P.M., 10:00 P.M., and 12:00 midnight.

Note: There is no mandated dockside season, but the boat may remain dockside if weather is threatening.

Location: 18th Street
Mississippi Riverfront
Rock Island, IL 61201

Phone: 1-800-477-7747

Illinois Gaming Board

Illinois Gaming Board
160 North La Salle, Suite 300 South
Chicago, IL 60601
Phone: 312-814-4700

9

The Indiana Boats

Indiana legalized riverboat gambling in June 1993, becoming the sixth state to do so. The state has, as of this writing, limited the number of licenses it intends to grant to a total of eleven. These will be divided into three regions as follows: five licenses for areas to the northeast, bordering Lake Michigan,

five on the Ohio River, and one for Patoka Lake, which is near
French Lick in the south central part of the state, less than fifty
miles from the Kentucky border. There are also design restrictions on the Ohio River boats, which must be traditional in
design. The owners of the boats on Lake Michigan are free to
design their boats as they choose, providing that the boats are at
least 150 feet in length and are capable of carrying at least 500
passengers. Cruises will be limited to four hours, with dockside
gambling permitted for a maximum of thirty minutes prior to
departure and after return. In the case of bad weather, dockside
gambling is permitted. This issue gives rise to some interesting
questions and considerations. Who determines what constitutes
inclement weather? It is decidedly to the casinos' advantage, for
reasons already examined, that the boat be docked while gaming
is in progress. This issue has already been addressed in several
instances so far, with no clear resolution other than that the individual captain usually has the final say.

There are no state-imposed bet or loss limits, nor is there any
limitation on space which the boat may allot for gaming, as with
some other states. Indiana charges a 20 percent tax on casino
revenues as well as an additional $3 per head admissions tax.

The Indiana Gaming Commission can be reached at 317-233-
0044.

10

The Iowa Boats

Iowa was the first state to legalize riverboat gambling, in 1989, with the first boat opening for business in April 1991. At one time, Iowa had a total of seven boats in operation, but that number dropped as boats in other states with less restrictive laws came on line.

The first thing you will note when looking at the average monthly riverboat winnings in Iowa is that they are substantially lower than those of any other states. It seemed until recently that Iowa, while being bold enough to legalize riverboat gambling, then sought to keep people from gambling by so restricting the process that nobody could win or lose. The state saw to

The President Riverboat Casino, Davenport, Iowa

its apparent intentions by imposing a bet limit of $5 per wager, with a maximum loss per person limited to $200. To enforce the law, each passenger was issued a sheet with ten tear-off vouchers totaling $200. Each voucher was presented at the cashier cage in order to receive an equal amount of chips or tokens for use at the tables or machines. Once the gambler had spent his or her $200, that was it. It was against the law to share vouchers, even between spouses.

Iowa also originally restricted the amount of floor space available for gaming to no more than 30 percent of the total size of the boat. This was changed in 1994 to allow casinos to use as much space as they liked for gaming, providing everything else is in order. While tax revenues received by the state as a result of riverboat gambling are lower than those taken in by other states, the rate charged by the state of Iowa is one of the highest, at 20 percent. These heavy gaming restrictions initially caused Iowa to lose several of its original riverboats.

The severity of the original restrictions seemed counterproductive, and yet in retrospect, had the original provisions not been so restrictive, gaming would never have passed in the state of Iowa at all. It is only now, after several years, that the population of Iowa at large has accepted legalized gambling. As a result of this wider acceptance and major 1994 legal revisions, there are no longer restrictions governing dockside boarding hours, bar limits, and, most importantly, bet limits. Individual counties may now hold referendums determining for themselves whether or not they wish to have riverboat gambling. There are now even slot machines at most of the dog-racing tracks. As a result of this decisive and recent turnabout, Iowa is again one of the most important states on the riverboat gaming map, and the future looks very promising for casino operators, gaming enthusiasts, and the state and local treasuries. Iowa is a wonderful place, and the gaming patron from out of state will find the local population and casino employees to be extremely hospitable.

The games allowed on the Iowa riverboats are the standard games of craps, blackjack, roulette, and so on. Electronic games such as slot machines and video games are also allowed.

Despite Iowa's originally restrictive gaming laws, there was something to be said for limiting bets. While many do not care for the policy, it allows the fun and sport of gaming without the personal risk of unlimited wagering and serious loss. With a maximum single bet of $5 and a $200-per-day loss limit, an individual wasn't going to lose too much. Gaming, like many other activities, requires responsible behavior. Ultimately, as time has shown, common sense cannot be legislated, regardless of lawmakers' good intentions.

All Iowa boats are seaworthy and required by law to be cruising while gaming is underway. Weather conditions in Iowa, however, require a dockside season which generally runs November 1 through March 31. Dockside gambling is permitted during this time, provided that, during the regular cruising season, a riverboat has cruised at least one cruise per day for a minimum of one hundred days. Iowa originally did not allow patrons to wander in and board the boat whenever they like, even during the dockside season. Instead, passengers were permitted by law to board only at certain predetermined times. Fortunately, as a result of recent legislation, passengers may now come and go as they please while the boat is dockside.

Note: Schedules on all boats as well as admissions are subject to change without notice. Reservations are also recommended for all Iowa boats. Since all boats have toll-free numbers, it is worth the time to call while making plans. You must be at least 18 years of age to enter an Iowa casino.

Iowa Gaming and Racing Commission
Lucas State Office Building, 2nd Floor
Des Moines, IA 50319
Phone: 515-281-7352

Iowa Division of Tourism
Department of Economic Development
200 East Grand Ave.
Des Moines, IA 50309
Phone: 515-242-4705

Great River Road Association
Pioneer Building, Suite 1513
336 Robert St.
St. Paul, MN 55101
Phone: 612-224-9903

The River Road system parallels the Mississippi River on both sides, all the way from Canada to the Gulf of Mexico. For a free map and brochure on this exciting trip, call or write the above.

A toll-free call to the above number will provide the caller with important information on upcoming events, lodging, riverboat gambling, and general information on the Quad Cities, (Davenport and Bettendorf, Iowa, and Moline and Rock Island, Illinois).

President Riverboat Casino

The President Riverboat Casino is one of several riverboats currently operating in Iowa and is one of four riverboats operating under the President banner. The other boats are located in St. Louis, Missouri, Biloxi, Mississippi, and at King's Landing, in Tunica, Mississippi. President Casinos is a publicly owned company and is traded on NASDAQ and listed as PREZ.

The mammoth Iowa riverboat is advertised as the largest cruising riverboat casino in the world, a claim made by several other boats in various states. This unique and authentic 297-foot sidewheeler was built in 1927 and is a registered national historic landmark. The boat has over 27,000 square feet of actual gaming space, including 700 slot and video machines, the largest number of 5 cent slots on the Mississippi, and 36 table games, including Wheel of Fortune, roulette, Red Dog, and several types of poker. The atmosphere of the boat is pleasant and festive, and the elegant antebellum decor evokes images of the grand riverboats of the classic era of riverboat gambling.

For a game of poker or a break from the action, passengers may retire to the quiet comfort of the Winner's Lounge on the third deck, for cocktails and conversation. But whether enjoying the two full decks of casino action or the pleasures of a cruise down the Mississippi River, they will find the President Riverboat Casino to be one of Iowa's greatest attractions.

The boat, known as "the Big One," is located at President's Landing in Davenport, an area referred to as "the Mississippi Strip." This deluxe riverside area includes the Blackhawk Hotel (two blocks away), the beautiful Le Claire Park, and President's Landing. Strollers are serenaded by the President Riverboat's calliope as they leisurely enjoy the landscaped walkways. Nearby, downtown Davenport features the Riverside Mall, an arts, crafts, and antiques mall which offers everything from folk art and southwestern crafts to fine antiques, including English and Victorian, not to mention restaurants serving a wide variety of gourmet foods.

In addition to the casino, restaurant facilities include the 250-seat Garden Cafe and the Mark Twain Lounge, both of which are located at the dockside facility.

Club: The President has its own in-house club called the Captain's Club. This club offers free membership, ID cards, and various discounts on goods and services.

Admission: At the time of this writing, all cruises are free Monday through Friday, with the exception of the Friday 5:00 P.M. and 9:00 P.M. cruises, which are $5 each. On Saturday the 8:00 A.M. cruise is free, but the others are all $5, except for the 7:00 P.M. cruise, which is $7. On Sunday the 1:00 P.M. and 5:00 P.M. cruises are $5 each, while the others are free. As always, call for prices and schedules, since both are subject to change without notice.

Cruise Schedule:

Sunday	9:00 A.M.	1:00 P.M.	5:00 P.M.	9:00 P.M.
Monday	8:00 A.M.	12:00 P.M.	5:00 P.M.	9:00 P.M.
Tuesday	8:00 A.M.	12:00 P.M.	5:00 P.M.	9:00 P.M.
Wednesday	8:00 A.M.	12:00 P.M.	5:00 P.M.	9:00 P.M.
Thursday	8:00 A.M.	12:00 P.M.	5:00 P.M.	9:00 P.M.
Friday	8:00 A.M.	12:00 P.M.	5:00 P.M.	9:00 P.M.
Saturday	8:00 A.M.	12:00 P.M.	3:30 P.M.	7:00 P.M. 10:30 P.M.

Note: A dockside season exists November through March. During this period the boat is docked due to weather conditions. Dockside gaming is permitted during this time.

Location: 130 West River Drive
               Davenport, IA 52801
  Phone: 1-800-BOAT-711

CLINTON

Clinton Convention and Visitors' Bureau
P.O. Box 1024
Clinton, IA 52733-1024
Phone: 319-242-5702

A call to the above number will provide the caller with up-to-date tips on lodging, gaming, local points of interest, and other travel-related information. The Convention and Visitors' Bureau will also gladly send information on the many various monthly events and activities.

Clinton Art Association
Gallery: 708 25th Avenue South
Mailing: P.O. Box 132
Clinton, IA 52732
Phone: 319-243-3300, 242-8055

For more than twenty-five years, the Clinton Art Association has served the area as a nonprofit organization dedicated to encouraging creativity and appreciation of the arts. As such, the association is involved in a number of annual and ongoing projects, including lectures, classes, and artist receptions. For more information contact the above.

Clinton, Iowa, is a small, picturesque town located on the western bank of the Mississippi. Named for nineteenth-century New York governor De Witt Clinton, the town developed from an area originally named New York. The city of Clinton and the Mississippi River have always been important to each other. Between 1850 and 1900 Clinton became the sawmill capital of America. Large logs were floated down the river from Minnesota and Wisconsin, milled in Clinton, and then sent to the rest of the country by river and rail. By 1892 lumber production had reached 195 million board feet. By 1900, however, the forests to the north were depleted, and the sawmills closed, causing Clinton to lose a quarter of its population almost overnight. Clinton recovered over time, and now has a population of roughly 50,000.

Clinton boasts a number of stately Victorian mansions built during the heyday of the sawmills, as well as other buildings of architectural interest. The 1914 Van Allen Department Store, for example, was designed by noted American architect Louis Sullivan, and has been restored and serves as a museum, archive, center for learning, and civic center.

Clinton also offers art galleries, a nationally recognized symphony, a community concerts series, and a variety of recreational sports and activities. The Eagle Point Nature Center, Bickelhaupt Arboretum, and Clinton County Historical Society are also worth investigating.

There are many excellent opportunities for shopping in Clinton, including a number of antique stores and shopping malls. The Historic Lyons Shopping District has several restaurants, craft and hobby stores, antiques,and a beauty shop.

There are also plenty of good restaurants, with everything from well-known chains, such as Wendy's, Long John Silver's, and Pizza Hut, to the Carousel, Rastrelli's, the Unicorn, and Yen Ching.

The presence of riverboat gambling has created an increased demand for hotel and motel rooms, a need which has been answered by the construction of a number of well-known national chains, such as Best Western and Ramada.

Clinton's Department of Parks and Recreation offers year-round recreational activities, with over one hundred programs. There are seventeen city-operated parks with a total area of over 475 acres, including ballfields, boat ramps, lighted tennis and softball courts, hiking and biking trails, outdoor basketball courts, and open-air shelters. For specific information on parks and activities, call 319-243-1260.

Eagle Point Nature Society
Box 95
Clinton, IA 52733-0095
Phone: 319-242-9088

Bickelhaupt Arboretum
340 South 14th St.
Clinton, IA 52732
Phone: 319-242-4771

Clinton County Historical Museum
Root Park off 25th Avenue North
Clinton, IA 52733
Phone: 319-242-1201

Mississippi Belle II

The Mississippi Belle II, located in Clinton, formerly a day cruise
boat, is owned by River Rides, in Dubuque, and is the second
Mississippi Belle. The first Mississippi Belle, originally known as
the Quad City Queen, was recently sold to a company in St. Louis
which will continue operating this boat as a casino. The 600-pas-
senger boat opened in June 1991 and has a total of 260 slot and
video machines, 9 blackjack tables, 1 roulette wheel, 1 craps
table, 3 seven-card Stud tables, and 1 Texas Hold 'Em. There is a
gift shop on board, as well as a restaurant which features a $7.50
lunch and $9.95 prime rib.

A new boat designed by Kehl Riverboats, Inc., opened in September 1994, replacing the smaller Mississippi Belle II, which
moved to the Burlington–Fort Madison area. The new boat was
constructed by Houma Fabricators in Houma, Louisiana, and
measures 228 by 64 feet. It has four decks and holds 1,000 passengers and a crew of 250. Built at a cost of $13 million, the boat
is powered by two 580-horsepower Cummins engines and is
equipped with a Cummins 200-horsepower bow thruster.

The larger boat offers expanded casino space, with a total
gaming area of 10,577 square feet which includes 518 slot
machines, 20 blackjack tables, 2 craps tables, 1 roulette wheel,
and a private poker room with 4 tables. There is a 325-seat dining room, a stage for live entertainment, a child care room, three
bars, and a medical room. The fourth deck is open air for scenic
cruising.

Note: A dockside season exists November 1 through March 31.
During this period, the boat is docked due to weather conditions.
Gaming is permitted dockside during this time, between the

hours of 9:30 A.M. and 1:30 A.M. Reservations are suggested, and you must be 18 to enter the casino. The casino offers specialty group cruises as well as cruise and dining packages. Call for further information and specific boarding times.

Club:	No club at time of writing
Admission:	No admission charge during dockside season. For cruise prices, see below.
Hours of operation:	Dockside (November through March), 9:30 A.M.–1:30 A.M.

Cruises (May through October):	Board	Depart	Admission	
	9:30 A.M.	11:00 A.M.	$5.00	
	1:30 P.M.	3:00 P.M.	$5.00	
	5:30 P.M.	7:00 P.M.	$5.00	$7.95 (Saturday only)
	9:30 P.M.	11:00 P.M.	$5.00	

Location:	Showboat Landing, Riverview Park Clinton, IA 52733
Phone:	1-800-457-9975

DUBUQUE

Dubuque Diamond Jo

The Dubuque Diamond Jo opened in April 1994, is owned by the Greater Dubuque Entertainment Company, and is a traditional two-story Victorian sidewheeler. The 185-foot-by-46-foot craft was converted into its present casino configuration by the Ballinger Company, in Harvey, Louisiana. Prior to that time, the original and smaller boat had served as an area excursion boat. The boat now has a capacity of 750 passengers and approximately 10,000 square feet of actual gaming space. The casino has 320 slots, 13 blackjack tables, 1 roulette wheel, and 2 craps tables.

The dockside facility is a two-story brick building which serves as a holding area for waiting passengers, as well as housing food and beverage services. Banquet and party rooms are also located dockside and are available for special functions. Call for details.

Club: A players' club exists with various discounts and merchandise available. Membership is free. Call for information.

Admission: Prices vary depending upon season and time of cruise. Senior discounts are available. Prices range from free to $7.

Hours: The boat sets out on its first cruise at 8:00 A.M. and is always back for the night by 1:30 A.M. Each cruise lasts about 2 hours and covers a total distance of about 20 miles. *Note:* As with all Iowa boats, a dockside season exists from November through March.

Location: 3rd Street Ice Harbor
Dubuque, IA 52004

Phone: 1-800-LUCKY-JO

Spirit of Dubuque (Nongambling excursion boat)

The Spirit of Dubuque is a nongambling, 377-passenger excursion boat owned by Roberts River Rides, operators of the gambling riverboat Mississippi Belle II. The Coast Guard–inspected stern-wheeler is a double-decked boat which features lunch, dinner, and sightseeing cruises.

Open: May through October

Location: 3rd Street Ice Harbor
Dubuque, IA 52004

Phone: 1-800-426-5591

SIOUX CITY

Sioux City Sue

Sioux City Sue, the only boat located on the Missouri River, was just sold to Gamma International, and at the time of this writing will be leaving Iowa for a destination as yet unannounced. There will, however, be a newer and larger boat taking its place.

PART III

HOW TO PLAY, WIN, AND HAVE FUN

11

Take a Chance

T he following games are found in the majority of riverboat casinos, but some may vary. Whatever game you choose, you'll be sure to have loads of fun. The following will give you an idea of how the more popular casino games work. Tips on how to make your money last longer follow the explanation of each game.

SLOT MACHINES

Not so many years ago, all the slot player had to do was insert a coin, pull the handle, look at the middle line to see whether a winning combination had come up, and collect any coins that spilled into the tray below.

Harrah's Casino, Vicksburg, Mississippi

Now, although most traditional-style slot machines still have handles, many of them are computerized. They have bars, which you can push to activate the reels (most of them have handles as well, as studies found that many gamblers felt they had more "control" of a machine when they pulled the handle). Instead of spitting out the coins, contemporary machines often tally up their total under a readout that says "Credits," and the player must push a button called "Collect" in order to retrieve those coins.

In addition to the traditional three-reel machines, there are also machines with four and five horizontal reels. Today's symbols are a far cry from the oranges, plums, and bells that date back to the early days. You'll still find the fruit-and-bell machines, to be sure, but they've been joined by sevens in various colors (some of them even licked with tongues of fire to show how hot they are); bars with gemstones on them; Olympic gold, silver, and bronze "medals"; hot-air balloons that float up if they stop one space below the payline; "wild" symbols in a variety of guises; and logos of the various casinos which when lined up in a row mean the club's super jackpots.

The machines make slurping noises and play tunes when winning combinations are hit. Some of them even talk to the players, though their vocabularies are limited.

As far as the play is concerned, the most important difference in today's machines is that more likely than not, they have multiple paylines (ways in which winning combinations can occur). When the newer machines have a single payline, they require that multiple coins be played in order to collect the posted awards should certain symbols appear on that payline.

The payout for each machine and coin requirements are listed on its front. It's imperative that you take a few moments to look at this information before you insert any coins. I cannot tell you how many times I have seen gamblers insert one dollar token and miss collecting on the $100 jackpot that requires $3 to win.

The most common multiple-coin machines are:

One-Way. There is only one horizontal payline, but payout increases for each additional coin played. The majority of these are two- or three-coin machines. Most of the payout increases are proportional, but the full complement of coins must be played in order to win the jackpots on some machines or the super jackpots on others. Generally, those super jackpots pay out about four times the amount that one would win with one less coin inserted, i.e. one $1 token, $200; two $1 tokens, $400; three $1 tokens, $1,600.

Three-Way. There are three parallel paylines, each reading horizontally from left to right. Winning combinations on any of the lines pay out if three coins have been played.

Five-Way. Three horizontal paylines and two diagonals, going from left bottom to right top and left top to right bottom. Winning combinations on any of the lines pay out if five coins have been played. The fifty-line jackpot is substantially larger than those on other lines.

Smaller jackpots are paid out automatically by the machines. Larger ones may pay a certain number of coins automatically and the balance is paid by an attendant, or the entire amount may be hand paid. If you hit a jackpot and all of the coins are not disbursed by the machine, do not play the machine off until an attendant gives you the rest of your winnings.

Maximizing Your Money

Payouts vary from machine to machine. Identical-looking slots in the same casino may pay amounts that are different from each other on winning combinations—especially on their jackpots. Therefore, it's a smart idea to look around before you start playing. If the machines have the same number of symbols on their reels in the same combinations (and most identical machines do), you'll have a better chance on those with the higher payouts.

Some casinos advertise a 99 percent payback on certain machines, and they are required by law to tell the truth about this. What the 99 percent figure means is that over a prolonged period of time the machine pays back 99 cents on the dollar.

However, this does *not* mean that if you put $100 in a machine you will get $99 back. Or that you'll get at least $990 back on a $1,000 investment. You might get $990 or you might get $3,000 or you might get $255.

Remember, you'll be paid for winning combinations which appear on lighted lines only, so be sure that your coins register as you put them in (sometimes the receptors are not working properly and fail to accept every coin, dropping them into the tray instead).

Obviously, the greater the number of reels, the more difficult it is to line up symbols all of the same kind or in a certain sequence; hence, the higher payouts (Megabucks and Quarter-mania are both four-reel machines). And generally, the more different symbols a machine has on its reels, the more difficult it is to line up the big wins, since more nonwinning combinations are possible.

Lots of slot machines have chairs attached or placed in front of them. While it may add to your comfort to sit while you play, that comfort also entices you to stay at a machine longer. If you really don't want to gamble for more than a few minutes, stand up.

VIDEO POKER

Extremely popular, these computerized games can be found in just about every casino. Supposedly the most addictive of any of the coin machines, what makes them so intriguing is that there's a decision-making element involved that's missing from slot machines.

The first machines, introduced about twenty years ago, were regular draw-poker machines. Since then, variations such as Deuces Wild, Jokers Wild, and Deuces and Jokers Wild have been added.

The basic concept of the machines is the same as that of draw poker as played in poker rooms. The object is to get the best hand possible in two tries, the deal and the draw.

In most cases, if you choose to play a 25-cent machine which returns bets on a pair of jacks or better, you will be able to play for an hour or more on a $20 investment. The length-of-time-played/money-spent ratio is much more to the player's favor than that of the slots, for example, where the typical grind rate on multiple-coin nickel machines has been estimated at $25 an hour, on dime machines, about $50 an hour, and approximately $125 on quarter machines.

The first step to winning at traditional video draw poker is choosing the right kind of machine. Almost all of the machines return bets on a pair of jacks or better—which, if you play correctly, allows you to play lots of hands on a roll of coins. And the more plays you get for your money, the more chance you have of hitting winning combinations.

Payout rates vary considerably. Most likely, the best you'll see for single-coin bets on regular video poker machines with the pair-of-jacks-or-better feature are as follows:

Royal flush	250 coins (five coins pays $1,000)
Straight flush	50 coins
Four of a kind	25 coins
Full house	9 coins
Flush	6 coins
Straight	4 coins
Three of a kind	3 coins
Two pairs	2 coins

You'll be more apt to find machines that pay eight coins for a full house and five for a straight. If payouts are any lower than this, keep looking—even if you have to go to another casino.

On machines that don't pay on a pair of jacks or better—and they're becoming rare—royals, three of a kind and two pairs usually pay the same as above, but the other combinations pay slightly to decidedly more. A straight flush commonly pays 100 coins; four of a kind, 40; full house, 10; flushes, 7; and straights, 5.

Almost all the machines pay a big premium for hitting a royal flush when the maximum number of coins is played. For instance, on a five-coin quarter machine, you could win $250 on four coins played, but $1,000 if all five coins were inserted.

Before you start to play, look closely at the buttons on your machine. On most machines, square buttons placed directly under each card say "Hold." But on certain machines (they're definitely in the minority), those buttons say "Discard." Other buttons on the machine say "Deal", "Draw" (the deal/draw function is usually, but not always, performed by a single button), "Cancel," "Stand," and "Collect." These buttons are not in the same order on all makes of machines. And you can lose money if you press the wrong one.

As coins are inserted into the slot, the payback rates for the various winning combinations will appear on the video screen above the playing area, increasing proportionally with the insertion of each coin (except in the case of the royal flush, as mentioned above). Machines take from one to five, eight, or ten coins.

In some casinos, a group of video poker machines may be linked together, with a computerized readout above the bank of machines, which adds to the progressive jackpot each time coins are put into any of the machines.

After the money is inserted, the player presses the Deal button and five cards appear on the screen. The player chooses the cards he or she wishes to hold (or discard, if the machine plays that way) and presses the appropriate buttons. On some older-model machines, the Cancel button can be used when the wrong buttons have been pushed; on later-model machines, pushing a button the second time negates the first.

When the player has made the choices, he or she presses the Draw button, which causes the unwanted cards to disappear from the screen and others to take their places. In the case you're dealt a "natural" (a winning combination such as a royal, flush, straight flush, four of a kind, full house, flush, or straight), press the Stand button and you'll be paid. On machines without this button, it will be necessary to press the Hold buttons under each of the five cards. On most later-model machines, when a royal is hit and maximum coins played, the coins are automatically registered as soon as the combination is hit.

You can play from 10 to 15 games a minute, depending upon how fast the coin-receiving action and payout are on a particular machine and how long you spend deciding which cards to keep. If you play nonstop, that means 600 to 900 games per hour.

According to officials of IGT, one of the leading video poker machine manufacturers, the inner workings of the machines use a pseudo-random number generation and each new game involves a deal from all 52 cards in the deck. If this is so, these are your chances of being dealt the various winning combinations:

Pair of jacks or better	1 in 2.4
Two pairs	1 in 21
Three of a kind	1 in 47
Straight	1 in 255
Flush	1 in 509
Full house	1 in 694
Four of a kind	1 in 4,165
Straight flush	1 in 72,193
Royal flush	1 in 649,740

Despite what the company people say, experienced video poker players are convinced that these combinations come up far more often.

In Deuces Wild video poker, the 4 twos are wild, which makes winning combinations come up far more often than in the traditional computer game. Payouts, as a result, are less. Look for machines with these payouts on one coin.

Royal flush without deuces	250 coins (5 coins pays $1,000)
Four deuces	200 coins
Royal flush with deuces	25 coins
Five of a kind	15 coins
Straight flush	9 coins
Full house	3 coins
Flush	2 coins
Straight	2 coins
Three of a kind	1 coin

In the Joker Poker game, there's one joker added to the 52-card deck, and the best payout rates look like this:

Royal flush, without joker	500 coins (5 coins pays $1,000)
Five of a kind	200 coins
Royal flush, with joker	100 coins
Straight flush	50 coins
Four of a kind	20 coins
Full house	10 coins

Flush	6 coins
Straight	5 coins
Three of a kind	2 coins
Two pair	1 coin
Kings or better	1 coin

Machines with both jokers and deuces wild offer the lowest payouts. However, the jackpot for hitting all four deuces plus the joker with all five coins played is $4,000 on some 25-cent machines—as high as you'll find for many video poker machines that take dollar tokens.

Maximizing Your Money

Look for Jokers Wild machines that return your bet on a pair of kings and higher, or at least on a pair of aces.

To further tip the odds in your favor, here's a rundown of the mistakes typical unsuccessful players make:

1. Talking to friends while playing, and taking their advice—no matter how bad it may be. This is okay if your object is having a good time without caring whether you win or not. But to maximize profits, you really have to pay attention to what you're doing in this game.
2. Playing hunches. An example would be holding a single low card just because it's your lucky number, rather than hanging on to a face card which, if paired, will give you another shot at a bigger payout.
3. Bucking the odds. Examples: holding three nonconsecutive low cards of the same suit instead of two kings, drawing to an inside straight when you could hold a pair, taking the big chance consistently rather than settling for a smaller payback on a sure thing.
4. Playing when you're tired. If you're not alert, you'll make mistakes, and there's nothing worse than accidentally pressing the Draw button rather than standing when the machine has cooperated by dealing you four of a kind.

"21" (BLACKJACK)

Two cards are dealt face-down to each player by the dealer. The dealer's first card faces up; the second, down. The object of the game is to hold cards that total 21 or come closer to 21 than those held by the dealer. The king, queen, and jack each count as 10. The cards from two to ten are counted at their face value. An ace can be counted either as 1 or 11.

An ace with any king, queen, jack, or ten is called a blackjack. If you're dealt this combination, turn your cards face-up immediately and the dealer will pay you one and a half times your bet, unless the dealer also has a blackjack. In this case, no money or chips change hands. When the dealer's and player's cards total the same amount, it's called a push.

If you aren't dealt a blackjack, you may want the dealer to "hit" you (deal you another card). You may be dealt as many cards as you want, one at a time, so long as your cards don't total more than 21. If the total goes over 21, you "go bust" and lose. In this case, you turn your cards face-up. When you do not want to be hit, you may "stand" by sliding your cards face-down under your bet.

After all the players at a table either have their cards in a stand position, have been dealt a blackjack, or have gone bust, the dealer turns his or her down card face-up and stands or draws more cards as necessary. The dealer must draw to any count up to and including 16 and stand on 17, except a "soft" 17 (any combination of cards containing an ace, but not a ten, that totals 17). When the dealer has a soft 17, the dealer must draw.

CRAPS

Granted, the craps table layout looks pretty complicated. But in reality it's a fairly simple game. In each game, one of the players is the "shooter." The shooter begins a pair of dice in what is called the "come-out roll." On that roll, when the shooter rolls a 7 or 11, he or she (and the bettors who bet with the shooter) wins. If the shooter rolls craps (a 2, 3, or 12) the shooter (and those who bet with him or her) loses.

When any of the other totals (4, 5, 6, 8, 9, or 10) come up, that number becomes the established point and the shooter has to continue rolling the dice until he makes that number again in order to win. However, if the shooter rolls a 7 before he or she makes a point, the player "sevens out" and loses.

The bets you can make follow:

Pass Line. This is what you play if you're betting with the shooter—that he will roll a 7 or 11 on the come-out roll; that he won't roll a 2, 3, or 12. When the point is established—remember, that's a 4, 5, 6, 8, 9, or 10—the shooter must roll it again before he throws a 7.

Don't Pass. You're betting against the shooter on this one, so you'll win if he or she rolls 2, 3, or 12 on the come-out. You'll lose if the shooter throws a 7 or 11, and if the shooter rolls the established point before rolling a 7. As you can see, this bet is the exact opposite of the Pass. You are limited to one Pass/Don't Pass bet per roll.

Come. The same as the Pass bet, except that it can be placed only after a point is established.

Don't Come. The same as the Don't Pass bet, except that it can be placed only after a point is established. You can place as many consecutive Come/Don't Come bets as you like.

Place. A bet on any or all of the following: 4, 5, 6, 8, 9, 10 (Place numbers), says that the number or numbers betted on will be thrown before a 7.

The Field. A one-roll bet that a 2, 3, 4, 9, 10, 11 or 12 will be rolled. If a 5, 6, 7, or 8 is rolled, the bet is lost.

Big Six and Big Eight. You can make this bet on either or both of these numbers at any time. You win if the number(s) you choose is rolled before a 7 is thrown.

Hard Way. This bet says that the number you have chosen (it must be an even number) will be made by rolling the dice so that the same number is up on each, i.e. two 6's for a 12.

There are still other bets you can make, but it's a good idea to stick to the basics until you have had a fair amount of hands-on experience. Even then, you may decide to limit your wagering to Come and Pass bets, since they give you a much better chance of winning the others.

Maximizing Your Money

Sometimes when you're playing, you may be "on a roll." The mistake is to think that roll will last for three more hours. When you get a reasonable amount ahead, be prepared to cash in your chips as soon as your luck starts turning.

KENO

To play, mark from one to fifteen of the eighty numbers on a keno ticket. You'll find these tickets in areas with counters and desklike seats called keno lounges. the next step is to take your ticket to the counter and give it to a keno writer, who will copy the ticket and write the amount of your bet in the margin. The minimum amount you can bet is one or two dollars.

Each game is assigned a number in sequence, and tickets must be purchased prior to the time the game is closed. During the course of the game, eighty ping-pong type balls, numbered from 1 to 80, are mechanically agitated in a plastic or wire container. One by one, twenty of these balls are ejected and their numbers are illuminated on keno flashboards throughout the casino.

Whether you win or not depends upon how many of the numbers marked on your ticket light up on the keno board. Also, your ticket number must correspond to the game number on the lighted board. If you play a five-spot ticket (five numbers marked), for example, at least three of those numbers must come up. On a ten-spot ticket, you must "catch" at least five.

A variation, called the Way Ticket, allows playing two or more combinations of numbers on a single ticket. Diagrammed explanations of how Way Tickets work are available in most keno lounges.

Another keno variation is called 20/40 keno. After the first twenty balls are mechanically expelled, twenty more are ejected. Players who buy forty-ball cards are paid when a certain number of their numbers are caught (or conversely, when none—or only a specified low number of them—come up).

If you want to play keno while eating in a casino restaurant or having a drink at the bar, keno runners will take your tickets and money to the counters for you—and bring you your winnings (be sure to tip when you win).

Maximizing Your Money

The house edge in keno is the highest of any of the games. This would make it one of the least attractive except for the fact that it is also the slowest game, so your money disappears at about the same per-hour rate.

The eight-spot is one of the most popular tickets to play, since it pays the highest jackpot for the least number of correct selections—$50,000 when all eight numbers are caught. But you will find that when you catch four of your numbers, you only get your money back, and catching half the numbers when the odds are one in four is a feat in itself.

Before you decide to play keno for money, play twenty or more "make-believe" games. Fill out the tickets, but don't bring them to the ticket counter. Then, after each game, write down the money you would have spent and the money you would have won. The odds are very good that you'll be happy you didn't play for cash.

After all this, if you *must* play a game, check over all your used tickets to see if any numbers came up an abnormally large percentage of the time. Then mark a card with those numbers only (there probably won't be more than two or three of them if there are any) on the chance that there's something about the composition of certain of the numbered balls that's causing them to be ejected more often than the others. If that doesn't work—and even if it does—play your "favorite" numbers a couple of times, then find some other game to play. In most cases, you will have spent a couple of hours with far less of a loss than you would have if you had been playing all those games for real.

POKER

The two most commonly played poker games are Seven-Card Stud and Texas Hold 'Em. Red Dog is popular too. If you don't play poker regularly, don't even think about playing in a casino.

These are the big boys. Many of them make their living gambling. Play can be very fast, and there's no place for the novice or for anyone who can't afford to lose a lot of money in a very short time.

Maximizing Your Money

There are four variations on poker played at casino tables (rather than in the poker room) which you can play for generally lower stakes and which don't move as fast. Three of the games—Sic Bo, Fan Tan, and Pai Gow—have Chinese origins. The fourth, Caribbean stud—is a newcomer which is fast becoming popular.

Sic Bo. This is an ancient Oriental game centering around three die in a sealed shaker. About fifty possible bets can be placed on the table layout. They include the various numbers that all three die will total when tossed, and the combinations of numbers that can occur.

Fan Tan. Players place their bets on a square board with numbered sides (1, 2, 3, and 4) or on areas at the corners between the numbers. When all bets are placed, the dealer removes a portion of a pile of beans which are concealed by a brass bowl. When the beans are exposed, the dealer divides the beans with a thin wand into rows of four until only 4, 3, 2, or 1 bean remain. The number of beans remaining determines which are the winning numbers.

Pai Gow. Pai Gow is a complicated game played with 32 specially designed dominoes, and errors in playing result in disqualification, so the game is patronized mostly by Orientals who have played it for years. Pai Gow *poker*, however, is a table game that's become popular with Orientals and Occidentals alike. A combination of Pai Gow and poker, it is played with an ordinary deck of 52 cards plus one joker. The joker is used as an ace or to complete a straight or flush.

Players are dealt seven cards each, which are then arranged into two hands. One hand contains five cards and is called the high hand. The second hand contains two cards and is known as the low hand. The object of the game is to win the bet by having both the high and low hands rank higher than the respective hands of the banker. The ranking is determined by traditional poker rules. If both hands rank lower, the wager is lost to the banker. If either hand wins while the other loses, the wager is a "push" and no money changes hands. The house handles all bets and charges a 5 percent commission on all winning wagers.

Caribbean Stud. This is a beat-the-dealer game played at a table much like those on which 21 is played. Players receive five cards face-down and the dealer receives four cards face-down and one card up after bets have been placed by each player in his or her "ante box."

To participate in the progressive jackpot (a payout to players who have any of the winning poker combinations such as three of a kind or a full house), players must drop dollar tokens into the slots in front of their ante boxes.

If a player thinks his or her hand cannot beat the dealer's hand, the player folds and loses his or her ante bet. If the player thinks his or her hand will beat the dealer's hand, the player must place a bet of exactly twice the amount of the ante bet to call the dealer.

Dealer must have an ace/king or higher to continue. If the dealer cannot open with at least ace/king, the hand is over. The dealer collects the cards and pays even money on all the ante bets of players who did not fold.

If the dealer's hand is high enough to open, and the player's hand is higher, the player will be paid even money on the ante bet and a bonus amount on the call bet, ranging from 2 to 1 to 100 to 1.

AND THERE ARE MORE ...

COMPUTERIZED "21" MACHINES

After inserting coins (usually 25-cent or $1 tokens), the player presses the Deal button. Two dealer cards appear at the top of the screen, one face-up and the other face-down. Below are the player's two cards, both face-up. If the dealer's two cards total 21, the second card flips face-up and the game is over with the player losing (some "21" machines return the coins in case of a tie). If the dealer's cards total less than 21, the player has the option of pressing the Hit button for an additional card or cards. If the total reaches more than 21, the game is over and the player loses. When the player is satisfied with a hand, he or she presses the Stand button, at which time the dealer's hidden card is exposed. If the dealer has 17 or more points, he must stand. Otherwise, additional cards are dealt. If the player's total is closer to 21 than the dealer's, the player receives double his or her money from the machine. Just play this one as you would if you were in a game with a live dealer.

COMPUTERIZED KENO

The player inserts a coin, presses the Erase button, then, with a pointer attached to the left front of the machine, "marks" the eighty-number playing board on the screen with the numbers he or she wishes to play. One to ten numbers can be marked on most machines. As the numbers are marked, the number of catches required to win appears with their respective payouts on an upper screen. As soon as the Play button is pressed, twenty numbers are illuminated in rapid succession on the playing board. As each of the player's numbers is "caught," it's indicated by a check mark.

Maximizing Your Money

This is another game that's extremely hypnotic. Play takes only seconds, and most machines can gobble up to five coins per game. Since the odds are heavily weighted in favor of the house, those quarters can go very fast, and it's possible to lose more than $50 in quarters in a half hour.

ROULETTE

The roulette wheel has thirty-six numbers from 1 to 36 marked on it, plus an "0" and "00." The numbers are alternately colored red and black, but the 0 and 00 are green. When the players have placed most of their bets by putting their chips on the layout containing all the numbers plus combinations of numbers and odd/even number options, the dealer spins a small white ball in the opposite direction of the spinning wheel. Bets may be placed until the ball is ready to leave the track and the dealer signals that betting is closed. The number above which the ball stops is the winner. Single-number wins, including 0 and 00, usually pay approximately 35 to 1. Odds vary with the combination bets.

Maximizing Your Money

Stay away from this one. The house advantage is about 5.25 percent—too high to make the game attractive to anyone wanting to stretch their casino dollars.

PM WHEEL

The Pari-Mutuel Wheel, sometimes called the Wheel of Fortune or Big Six, is a wheel of about a six-foot diameter. Bets are placed on a layout which corresponds to the money denominations displayed in various positions on the wheel. When all the bets are in, the dealer spins the wheel and the money winners are those who have bet on the denominations where the pointer comes to rest. On most PM Wheels, a bet on the $20 bill pays 20 to 1; $10 pays 10 to 1; $5 pays 5 to 1; $2 pays 2 to 1; and $1 pays even money.

Maximizing Your Money

Resist temptation on this one too.

BACCARAT

Baccarat (pronounced bah-kuh-*rah*) is the Americanized version of Chemin de Fer and is played with eight decks of cards, shuffled by the croupier and dealt from a box called the "shoe." Two hands of two or three cards each—called the "players" and the "bankers"—are dealt. Bettors can wager on either hand or on a tie. "Bank" bettors must pay the house a commission (usually 5 percent, but occasionally lower) on winning bets.

The object of the game is to come as close as possible to 9 points. All cards from ace through ten are counted at face value. Each face card has a value of 10. The cards in each hand are totaled, but only the last digit is used. For example, 10 plus 6 equals 16 (scored as 6). Nine plus 5 plus 10 equals 24 (scored as 4). Whether two or three cards are dealt to a hand depends on the following:

When player's hand holds two cards totaling:

0, 1, 2, 3, 4, 5	must draw third card
6, 7	must stand
8, 9	a natural; bank cannot draw

When banker's hand holds two cards totaling:

3	draws third card except when player's third card is 8
4	draws third card when player's third card is 2 through 7
5	draws third card when player's third card is 4, 5, 6, or 7
6	draws third card when player's third card is 6 or 7
7	must stand
8, 9	a natural; player cannot draw

Maximizing Your Money

This is a game that's enjoyable if you know the rules well enough to relax. If you don't, it's more fun than most casino games to watch. Above all, don't bet on ties—the house has a 14 percent edge on tie bets.

PART IV
THE
FUTURE

12

Just the Beginning

Where will it all end? There's really no telling. Kentucky recently announced that its lottery had added more than $400 million to its coffers during its first two years of operation. As a result of revenues like that, some states which had initially spurned gambling have reconsidered their positions. There is much speculation among investors that the casino craze

Star Casino, New Orleans, Louisiana

has just started and that eventually all states will have legalized gambling of some sort. Other, more conservative economists think that casino stock will be popular for a while and then will go bust, due to an oversaturation of the marketplace. One thing is certain, gaming is a $330-billion-a-year business already and continues to grow in all fields. Native American gaming, land-based casinos, state lotteries, and riverboats continue to become more acceptable, more appealing, and more common. So where will it end? It's an exciting question which remains, for the moment, unanswered.